"HOW TO BECOME AN
EXTRAORDINARY
MANAGER"

"HOW TO BECOME AN EXTRAORDINARY MANAGER"

Dr. Librado Enrique Gonzalez

"An average manager knows the answer, a good manager
measures the answer, but an Extraordinary Manager
predicts the question"

authorHOUSE®

AuthorHouse™
1663 Liberty Drive
Bloomington, IN 47403
www.authorhouse.com
Phone: 1-800-839-8640

First published by AuthorHouse   08/15/2011

ISBN: 978-1-4634-5300-8 (sc)
ISBN: 978-1-4634-5301-5 (ebk)

Printed in the United States of America

Any people depicted in stock imagery provided by Thinkstock are models, and such images are being used for illustrative purposes only.
Certain stock imagery © Thinkstock.

This book is printed on acid-free paper.

CONTENTS

ACKNOWLEDGMENTS

This book would not have been possible without the support and encouragement given to me by my family. To my wife, Lesley Paola, and my two daughters, Lesley Mireya and Meredith Daniela, I express my appreciation. Also, to my mother, Mireya Rosa Gonzalez, for her unconditional love all these years.

INTRODUCTION

Every organization needs great managers, and the individual that is able to delegate skills and responsibilities with ease, have the correct attitude and the ability to motive their employees, will be highly valued.

How do you become a great manager? How do you become a great leader? Are they even the same? To start off, let me clarify the differences that separate a manager from a leader. A leader provides vision and the motivational force to drive a project while a manager skillfully manages resources and juggles tasks essential for the success of the project. Leaders are proactive while managers are reactive. Leaders promote new directions while managers enable existing directions. In the future most companies will be looking for entrepreneurs to lead their organizations because they have graduated from Leadership School and they are ready to be the innovate force to create new markets while push forward to growing the company.

Having said that, both manager and leaders are actually quite similar, both in the terms of qualities exhibited as well as capabilities. They are not mutually exclusive to each other. A good manager can become a good leader, while a good leader must often perform managerial roles. Sometimes a good manager must even be both. The ultimate goal of a Leader is to become an Entrepreneur within the organization creating a culture of innovation and promoting the initiative to keep the business moving in the right direction.

So what does it require, in order to become an Extraordinary Manager? Common Sense in business (attitude and approach to issues-process); Judgment (decision making and believes); Planning (strategic and tactical); Organization (people and activities); Prioritization (important and urgent); Staffing (people and projects);

Delegating (skills and responsibilities); Supervising (objectives and processes); Measuring (results and progress); Reporting (facts and alternatives); and Innovation (vision and conviction).

In business as well as in life, attitude is everything. An Extraordinary Manager must consider all those elements to become a 100% business professional alone with a positive attitude in the things that he/she does and this rubs off on the employees over a period of time. Also, an Extraordinary Manager serves as a role model for his or her employees and this starts from having a great attitude.

Ultimately, an Extraordinary manager is somebody who can make the sum of team greater than a collection of individuals. Finally, an Extraordinary Manager allows the team to flourish and creates value to each individual as well as to the company.

Follow the steps and you will be at top before you ever know it.

CHAPTER I

Globalization

Globalization describes the process of regional economies, societies and cultures that have become a part of a global network of businesses. Globalization can be as simple as a business ordering some of its material from another country or as complex as housing corporate headquarters in one country, maintaining factories in another, and receiving parts or materials from yet another. The possibility of globalization has increased with the availability and global reach of the internet. Technological advances have played a key role in the increase of globalization, these days even a very small business with just one or two employees can be globalized. Globalization does not only pertain to business but government as well. Politics plays a key role in the globalized business.

The term globalization did not become popular until the 20th century. Then onwards, it has become a typical issue understood to affect the whole socio-economic and political life of states throughout the world. Besides, the discourse on globalization is complex with far reaching effects on national and international laws and policies pertaining to the social, economic and political matters

The increase of globalized business trade has created a global economy. This can have a positive impact on some countries and a negative impact on others. Countries with poor living conditions and poor wages experience an increase in wages and standard of living during the globalization process while the opposite is true for the countries that experience a high standard of living and high wages.

Countries on both extremities of the living standard range see the most dramatic economic changes.

There are several reasons for the increase in globalization over the years. The main reason is that labor and business operational costs are drastically cheaper in some countries. Countries with a lower standard of living typically have not addressed the need to protect the environment. For example, China has no regulations on the amounts of sulfur dioxide that is put into the air by manufacturing companies. People who live in China have a shorter life span so for obvious reasons are not as concerned with the long term ecological impact of their actions. China has been one of the countries that have experienced a dramatic increase in their standard of living. The increase in their standard of living is also increasing their life expectancies in recent years.

Globalization has many pros, here are some:

* Increases in economic productivity.
* Reduces prices for consumers.
* Gives developing countries access to foreign investment funds to support economic development.
* Transfers technology.
* Spreads democracy and freedom to countries while reducing military conflict.

But also, globalization has its cons, here are some:

* Causes job insecurity.
* Weakens environmental and labor standards.
* Prevents individual nations from adopting policies promoting environmental or social objectives, if these discriminate against products from another country.
* Wears down regional and national cultures and weakens cultural, linguistic, and religious diversity.
* Is compatible with dictatorship.

In order to properly be able to communicate within the world of globalization, individuals must understand the how labor forces influence international business. International business can be defined as business deals across national boundaries throughout the world. These deals are created and carried out to meet different client's needs and everything from labor quality to mobility effect, how well the client's needs are met. While the task of managing international business can be intimidating, with a little bit of research and understanding it can be very successful. Business managers must learn to manage polices, information technology systems, and be respectful of their host country's rules and regulations. International business managers must be able to look at the needed work force and determine the availability with their host country as well as the cost and level of skill needed.

Trading is the most common business within globalization, and is the one with the most amount of policies and regulations. A business manager with trading enterprises has to be aware of lots of policies and regulations, such as export controls and import controls. These controls are conformed of regulations such as quotas and tariffs. Quotas limit on the amount of goods that can be imported, and tariffs are taxes on imports. Another kind of regulation a manager has to be aware of is the antidumping duties. This regulation controls the sales of imported goods that are being sold at less than fair value. The most recent factor nowadays affecting in globalization, are international torts, this is another factor that managers should be aware of. All these policies and regulations are just a small part of what a manager should take in consideration when doing business in other countries, every manager should know what those policies mean and how it affects their own business, and if these policies are not respected the consequence is punishable by law.

Another important factor in international business, especially when you have industrial factories or companies in other countries, are the environmental and health regulations. As previously stated, some countries like China, don't have these kinds of regulations, but most countries do. A manager with industrial enterprises has to be very aware of what kind of regulations does the foreign or home country has, some regulations have to do with protecting the environment, pollution of air and water, toxic substances control, endangered species, conservation, and many more. All these policies and regulations if not respected are punishable by law.

The labor market is the relationship that workers and companies have. It constantly changes based on the supply and demand of labor.

When determining what labor is needed, business's want to find skilled workers at a low, manageable cost while skilled workers want to get the highest pay for their skills. Different factors that will determine how much a laborer should be paid are how much experience and education they have as well as their work ethics and quality of work. Outside influences can affect the price of labor as well. For example, if there is a high unemployment rate in the host country skilled workers can be obtained at a lower cost. Other factors are labor unions, high demand for workers, and the laws of the host country regarding wages.

Labor unions are another important factor when talking about a business. These unions are represented by the workers themselves and fight for the fair treatment of the workers in the companies, including wages, benefits, and working conditions. This is a delicate factor in international business because of the fact that all countries have very different laws and regulations in the matter. A manager has to respect the laws regarding employment at all times. If they have a company on another country they have to pay the wages based on the law of that country, and they also have to respect the demands of the unions in that country. As previously stated, if these policies and regulations are not respected or followed it is punishable by law.

Labor mobility is another important aspect. Labor mobility means changes to the location and conditions of workers across a set of jobs and physical space. Labor mobility will allow labor unions to improve the conditions of the employment including the wages, benefits, and work conditions. Labor unions will continuously fight to ensure workers are being treated fairly and have improved conditions. As a result from these changes the economic conditions will improve in the region. Minorities are important to utilize within the labor force as well. Discrimination of race, age, gender, etc. will not be tolerated and there are organizations to help prevent such within the workplace.

In conclusion, though there are the divided ideas as to how all states benefit from globalization, nowadays, most agree that issues in relations to human rights, environmental matters, etc, are the common concerns of international communities which have to be respected and promoted by the joint efforts in every corner of the world.

Moreover, since international business transactions are directly or indirectly related to these common concerns, it is believed to be a common concern as well. Therefore, laws of international business transactions have to be in a position to respect and promote principles and guide lines provided to regulate other global concerns. From this, it is easy to understand, how much the laws of international business directly or indirectly are under the influence of globalization and managers should be prepared for any future change that may come.

CHAPTER II

Legal Aspects for Managers due to Globalization

1. **Purpose**. The purpose of this chapter is to present the challenges that manager have in globalization. We first define globalization followed by legal, financial, cultural, and human resources aspects that managers should consider within the global environment.

2. **Definition of globalization**. The International Monetary Fund (IMF) staff defines economic globalization as "the increasing integration of economies around the world, particularly through the movement of goods, services, and capital across borders. The term sometimes also refers to the movement of people (labor) and knowledge (technology) across international borders. There are also broader cultural, political, and environmental dimensions of globalization." The IMF staff considers that the growth in global markets has helped to promote efficiency through competition and the division of labor and offer greater opportunity for people to tap into more diversified and larger markets around the world giving them access to more capital, technology, cheaper imports, and larger export markets. They emphasize that a core element of globalization is the expansion of world trade through the elimination or reduction of trade barriers, such as import tariffs. Greater imports offer consumers a wider variety of goods at lower prices, while providing strong incentives for domestic industries to remain competitive.

3. **Legal considerations**—The legal ramifications of the global markets are numerous. International organisms, international laws as well as local laws can be overwhelming. A practical initial approach would be to obtain a good international legal counsel, a top local legal firm and a local advisor or partner in each country that the manager intends to do business in.

   a. Global administrative law—Global Administrative Law (GAL) is an emerging field that contemplates regulation by administrative law-type principles such as transparency, accountability and review usually termed as "global governance". The scope has increased dramatically and presently there are over 2,000 intergovernmental organizations (IGO) and around 40,000 non-governmental organizations (NGO) throughout the world. To settle disputes, some regulatory entities have established judicial (or quasi-judicial) bodies, or other kinds of settlements such as negotiations. With the creation of these types of international organizations, the scope of traditional treaties among nations. Managers should be aware of world organizations, country and regional trade agreements, such as World Trade Organizations (WTO), International treaties between nations, such as the North American Free Trade Agreement (NAFTA), the Southern Common Market (Spanish Mercado Común del Sur—MERCOSUR), European Union, Asean Free Trade Area (AFTA), the Brazil, Russia, India and China (BRIC) country group, among others.

   b. Legal systems of the World—There are different approaches to law in the world.

      i. Common law, based on a legal tradition of precedent. The court cases become a precedent for future decisions on the same issue. This system is in effect in the United States of America and England.

      ii. Code law, where the specific laws are matched with situations. This system is not flexible to new situations where the rule of law has not been issued. It is practiced commonly in Europe.

      iii. Islamic law, where the law is based on the teachings of the Koran. This system is practiced in Islamic countries.

4. Socialist law, which is based on the premise that the government is always right. This system is practiced in former communist countries.

5. **Financial Considerations**—The globalization of the financial world is a tangible reality. There is presently an interdependency of the world's financial markets. The collapse of the subprime mortgage market in the United States had a worldwide effect on world markets leading to a global financial crisis. This is globalization at work.

   a. Worldwide Stock exchanges—The globalization of finance has enabled businesses to incorporate and raise capital on worldwide stock exchanges. The IMF staff reported that, "The world's financial markets have experienced a dramatic increase in globalization in recent years. Global capital flows fluctuated between 2 and 6 percent of world GDP during the period 1980-95, but since then they have risen to 14.8 percent of GDP, and in 2006 they totaled $7.2 trillion, more than tripling since 1995. The most rapid increase has been experienced by advanced economies, but emerging markets and developing countries have also become more financially integrated. As countries have strengthened their capital markets they have attracted more investment capital, which can enable a broader entrepreneurial class to develop, facilitate a more efficient allocation of capital, encourage international risk sharing, and foster economic growth."

   b. Monetary foreign exchanges—The increase of trade among nations due to globalization has impacted the value of the monetary foreign exchanges. The trade deficit of a country, i.e. when it imports more than it exports, reduces the value of its currency because there is less demand for it. On the other hand, when there is a trade surplus, i.e. when it exports more than it imports, the value of the currency increases because there is more demand for it. This reduced exchange rate makes exports more attractive in other countries, and imports less attractive. This is the global currency battle where countries want to maintain their currency rate low in order to increase their exports.

c. <u>International accounting standards</u>—There is a disparity in generally accepted accounting standards in the world. Each country would like to adopt its own standards. In an attempt to uniform these standards for a globalized environment, the International Accounting Standards Board has issued international accounting standards. Many countries have adopted these international accounting standards. The United States still have their own generally accepted accounting standards. Financial statements presented in different stock exchanges have to conform with the accounting standards that the specific country accepts.

d. <u>Tax considerations</u>—Taxes is a very complicated subject matter. Specific country corporation, import duties and payroll taxes, among others should be kept in mind when doing business in a global environment. As stated previously, local expertise is imperative.

6. **Cultural considerations**—Globalization has imposed a learning challenge for managers. They have to understand and immerse themselves in the culture of the country and to recognize the differences to be effective in a globalized cross cultural environment. On the other hand, cultural assimilations have been a direct result of globalization. Examples of these would be the presence of a McDonalds in front of the Louvre in Paris, and the proliferation of Starbucks in China, a tea drinking nation.

a. <u>Language differences</u>. There is a difference between the spoken and written language in business. For the spoken language, the first language is Mandarin with 845 million speakers, followed by Spanish with 329 million speakers and then English with 328 million speakers. However, English predominates on the Internet, and 35% of all the mail, telexes and cables are in English.
There are also regional differences in language, for example even though Spanish is spoken throughout Latin America, the meaning of a specific Spanish word differs from one country to another.

Anglo Saxon countries have a more direct approach to language, whereas latin and romance languages have a more indirect and flower type approach.

These differences would have a material impact if you were in a business meeting and were not aware of them.

b. Cultural differences—Gert Hofstede, a Dutch researcher, interviewed IBM executives in various countries, and found four key cultural differences:

i. *Individualism vs. collectivism*: The extent of individual responsibility vs group responsibility and reward. Indonesia and West Africa rank toward the collectivistic side. The U.S., Britain, and the Netherlands rate toward individualism.

ii. *Power distance*: The extent of separation of individuals based on rank. Power distance tends to be particularly high in Arab countries and some Latin American ones. Northern Europe and the U.S. rank lower.

iii. *Masculinity vs. femininity:* Values of competition and conquering are masculine, while values of harmony and environmental protections are feminine. Japan ranks high in more masculine countries, while the Netherlands rank low and the U.S. is close to the middle.

iv. *Uncertainty avoidance:* The extent of preference of structured situations with clear rules vs a preference of a more ambiguous one. Countries with lower uncertainty avoidance tends to be more tolerant of risk. Japan ranks very high, Britain and Hong Kong and the U.S. are lower.

7. **Human resources considerations**—Human Resource (HR) managers must adapt to the overall globalization requirements to combine linguistic, engineering and marketing knowledge. This is not an easy task to pinpoint individuals with this combination. They should promote cultural diversity by being familiar and understand other cultural norms. In a competitive international market, employees from diverse national backgrounds provide language skills and understanding of other cultures.

With information technology, globalization requires workplace flexibility. The 'virtual office' is characterized by creative and flexible work arrangements. More employees work off-site-up to two thirds of an organization in the 21st century. The HR manager would have to increase emphasis on performance and results and not on the traditional number of hours worked. In addition, off-site employees can expect to attend fewer physical meetings when there is the availability of video conferencing.

HR managers should take into consideration the cultural differences that shape managerial attitudes, when developing multinational management programs. Examples of this would be British managers value individual achievement and autonomy, French managers appreciate competent supervision, fringe benefits, security and comfortable conditions, and Indian managers give more importance of their culture and tradition.

8. **Conclusions.** Globalization is a very extensive subject. We attempted to present and list the challenges for managers in globalization to create an understanding of the various business aspects to be taken into consideration. Globalization is a continuous study of cross cultural, legal and financial impact of doing business in other countries in a constant changing environment.

CHAPTER III

Proactivity and tendencies at the workplace

Technology is changing, companies are changing, and politics are changing in other words the whole world is changing every day every minute. We are living in a very changeable world where transformation is common; and organizations are also victims of that variation. Markets are changing and is becoming more and more difficult for businesses to keep on track and fight on the market, that is why companies need to be aware of what is happening and predict what is coming in order to succeed. Managers need to be proactive and coach their employee to be as much proactive as they can; that will be the key of success.

Be proactive, do the things you can control and forget the ones you cannot; act in advance do not be reactive and wait for the things to happen. That is exactly what organizations are looking for today, proactive people. As Stephen covey mentions on his book the 7 habits of highly efficient people " Be Proactive is about taking responsibility for your life. You can't keep blaming everything on your parents or grandparents. Proactive people recognize that they are response-able"[1] It is not a matter of looking for excuses for what you did it is a matter of taking the responsibility of everything you do every step you take. In the workplace anything you do is going to affect the company that is why

---

[1]   "Books - 7 Habits of Highly Effective People - Habit 1: Be Proactive." *Dr. Stephen R. Covey*. Web. 02 May 2011. <https://www.stephencovey.com/7habits/7habits-habit1.php>

you need to know that any choice you make will have a consequence that you are responsible for.

Companies are looking for people who can predict and anticipate what is going to happen, they are not going to hire you for you to react to events and want for opportunities but to create them. Acting in advance will save the company a lot of money and will probably improve the performance that is why it is so important to change your attitude and become proactive in the workplace. Things will keep changing and companies need to be ready, they need to train all their workers toward the proactive philosophy.

Stephen Covey mentions on his book that there is a gap between stimulus and response, and is in that gap where we can find our potential to choose our response. There are four human endowments where we can find this power:

The first one is Self-awareness, which is basically to know that you have to choices of acting. The first thing a person needs to be clear is about them; they need to know that they have a choice between stimulus and response. At any situation in life you have to basic options, yes or no. If they are offering you something you can take or not, if somebody insults you then you can become angry or not. Not everyone is aware of that and most of the time they are very compulsive people, they are always reacting immediately without even thinking about their behavior. In business it is very important for you to know that difference because choices are everywhere, you need to take important decisions at any time and taking the right decision will depend on that. A proactive person points more towards his response rather than an active person who will follow his stimulus.

The second endowment is conscience, this refer to the ability you have to go back to your inner compass analyze the options you have and then decide what is right for you. This will also depend on the values the person has, his culture and personality. It is important to always based your decision in what you believe, in what you thing it is right. You need to be an ethic person at the workplace. People need to take in consideration their principles at any time they are taking a decision; the right thing to do will always be the best option.

Creative Imagination will also help you on decision-making process. In order to choose the best response it is important to have options. As many alternatives you have to the better your response will be. Proactive people create the options reactive people just wait for somebody to provide them with the options. Creativity plays and important role in creating the options because it is the tool that will help you to think and create them. People need to mentally generate several options in response when something happens. At the workplace it is very important to have several options because not all of them will work. The idea is to act in advance and have already other alternatives just in case one of them would not work.

The fourth one is independent will you need to decide on what you thing is right not in what people is expecting from you. Of course that what you think is right will be based on your principles but the thing is that you must act as who you are, what you like and what you think. Do not let other to decide for you, you are the only one who can decide. When the decision time comes you need to think about you, it does not matter what people is expecting from you to do, the only thing you need to do is to think about what you want and what you think is the best alternative to choose.

Reactive people often have a lack of one of those four factors that defined proactive people. As a proactive people you are able to combine the four of them and come up with opportunities and ideas than tend to be the best way. Managers need to be proactive need to have proactive people to work with in order to increase their productivity and become a great teamwork. "What matters is making the decision to start consciously directing your own life instead of being pushed along by external currents"[2]

Another important point for managers is to have a clear knowledge of any tendencies within their departments at all the time. When you are a manager and you have to coordinate several people under a department you need to know them and have clear what each of them is responsible for. As a manager you set the goals for each of them and then keep track of their job.

At the workplace anything you do will affect your productivity, how you do your job, how you relate to your co-workers, how you relate to your boss, everything. That is why manager should be aware of any tendency at her or his department. If they want to increase productivity they need to take care of those points.

---

[2]   Ibidem

Any situation can affect you even without you knowing you might be working less or doing things wrong because something happens to you. The idea of a good manager is to be aware of all those things and find a solution in order to help employees and increase their productivity. Even better will be for a manager as it was mentioned before to be proactive and try to eliminate any tendencies even before it happen. Manager must know their departments, any details of it and eliminate the room for things to happen because those things will affect the performance of the people on the department.

Your job as a good manager it is also to understand your subordinates and help them at any time. Sometimes employees are scare and prefer not to talk to their bosses and tell them what they want or even their opinion about something. I believe it is important to have a business relationship that will allow you both to interact and talk openly about any issue. As manager you need to do that because it will be easier for you to identify any tendency on your department. Working in a friendly environment will also eliminate conflicts between co-workers and even with you as a manager.

Involvement at the workplace is what any company is looking for, it is what a manager should do in order to create that atmosphere and make everyone feel comfortable. Obviously it needs to be some limits between subordinates and employees because sometimes they tend to confuse the situations and abuse. As manager you need to set the limits the best way possible. It is not about yelling and punishing, it is more about a business relationship where both parties known the limitation of it.

CHAPTER IV

The Importance of "Process" in Common Sense

It is no secret that everything in life involves or stems from a process. From getting up in the morning to flying a plane, everything has its required process. I find it important for me to clearly define the word process; process is defined as a series of actions bringing about a result. Now, why is process important to our common sense? Well, as I previously said, **everything** in life involves a process. In order to reach what will come to be our best common sense we need to first go through the process of getting there. We must never forget that good results come from a good process. This said, if our process of common sense is wrong, then the common sense that we make out of situations would be wrong as well. In order to have a good common sense we must start from the beginning, from the process itself. People tend to have the wrong idea that if you have a mistaken common sense is because something in you is wrong per se. This could not be further from the truth since people cannot be improved, made worst, or change; it is the process as a whole what improves and therefore, when the process changes you change. That is the importance of process in common sense. People need to stop trying to change everything about them when they or somebody else thinks a wrong decision has been made. They should know and focus on the real problem, which is what happened, how did they get to the wrong choice or decision in the first place? Every time that a bad decision is made, you should always sit clear-headed and look back on what you did that got you there. You probably won't be able to make the mistake disappear, but at least you'll know what to change and improve in order to make the best out of your common sense the next time.

Common Sense in the Professional Environment

'*Common sense is the least common of the senses*'—Horace Greeley (1811- November, 1872) Greeley's quote is not far from the truth. There are many different definitions of what common sense is, and yet it is difficult for many people to understand its real meaning. Aristotle Stated that common sense provides a point in which all senses come together, where the all the information is processed and the outcome of this would be available through conscience (qttd). For some religions, common sense may be defined better as the conscience of the people, the light or even as the voice of the Holy Spirit, something given by God to Human beings so that we can 'feel' what is right and wrong. However, all these statements somehow coincide in that common sense is something natural that allow us make choices and despite these choices are good or bad, what matters is how we fell about the choice we made, rather than the choice per-sé. This is precisely the reason why Scientifics are having issues to apply in Artificial Intelligence (AI) this moral capacity of valuing each decision and its possible reactions and emotions that this decisions can imply. As we all know, robotic is evolving at an incredible rate, and Human-like robots as we remember from the cartoons are starting to appear, but Scientifics are missing this Human touch. In other words, a solution to a certain problem may be logical and efficient, but inapplicable due to the moral consequences and emotional damages these decisions can bring along. Common sense allows us to distinguish which information is really reasonable, important and reliable among the data we receive daily (1,MRJ). The same concept is applied in Business Ethics: the Three R's (Respect, responsibility and results). Respect is something that must be applied to people, organizational resources and to the environment (1, Carson). Someone who has some common sense will know that lack of respect of any of these concepts can jeopardize the business, or at least the results will not end as expected. Responsibility to employees, coworkers, shareholders, customers, your organization and the image you project of yourself to others . . . at the time of decision making it is necessary to know the consequences that can come along with a rapid decision, and to assume the responsibility. This happens a lot with politician, during an interview there is no time to stop to think about and there is anybody who can help you answer properly; here to have a well developed common sense is crucial either to answer in a reasonable way or to follow up the consequences of an answer that was not so good. At this point we can see how common sense can fail sometimes and that is why common sense is just the basic piece of a whole. Having some level of success is not only due to good common sense. It goes from accepting frustrations, inconvenient, problems, to don't wasting money that you don't have yet; the truth is that despite our efforts sometimes there will be situations that we don't expect and that are out of our control (2007, Aguirre), if anything we will be left with experience and lessons for the future and this is however the way common sense is formed. Antonio Aguirre illustrates in his article 'Common sense in Business' a personal experience with a customer that shows us how CS can betray us:

—One gentleman went to his Office because he wanted to start a cold meat business. He was a lawyer already. The cold meat business was not his dream, but he had a 22 years old sun that he felt he had to help him out, so he decided to start this new business for his sun to manage with him. His sun had already 2 years that would wake-up every day a 4p.m. to play guitar with his friends and then go back to bed. The next day he would repeat the same process, making it a habit, or life style. The distress this gave to the father of tolerating the situation finally convinced him that his sun couldn't find a job, and it was his role as a father to help him out. However, one month later the business was ready, the father didn't think about losses and decided to start over with the better: he rented an excellent place in a small mall. After a couple of month the business started doing better and the father decided to close his other office to dedicate to his new business. Sadly, the business broke. The father put everything in a business he didn't know or had no experience and lost the job which not only supported his family all those year before, but also gave him the money to start this new business. His common sense as a father was to help out his son; that is what naturally every parent would want to do for his offspring. Since day 1 his son was not interested in improving his way of life. The common sense of the son was as basic as the common sense of the father, who just like Don Quixote of la Mancha, was fighting against the wind mills. This anecdote illustrates why in business is not enough to have basic common sense and to complement with judgment. Common sense is said to be natural, instinctive, the way we have been conditioned during our entire life by thing we've hear, read or experienced.

Common sense may help light the spark of many entrepreneurs when they visualize a new idea, a new concept that can have commercial acceptance, but many people are missing something else: good judgment. If we go only with what is natural in human beings we are going to fit only in the ordinary people area of the Venn diagram. If we want to succeed we have to offer something different, we have to see what ordinary people don't see. We must go beyond what is common and offer what is not common, to take all available resources to create something new, original, innovative. We want to fit in the extra-ordinary side of the diagram. Nevertheless, these two concepts cannot be apart. If you have only common sense, and you recognize only what is common this means that you are a common person. In the same way, if you are proficient at evaluating opportunities you need the common sense to recognize them.

Here is another real-life example that the Chinese author MA YI wrote in his book "Smart People know how to speak nicely" ("Chongminng ren hui shuo piaoliang hua"): The first time the French author Alexandre Dumas went to a little town in Russia, he decided to see the biggest book store in town. The owner of the town listened to this amazing news and decided to use this opportunity to leave a good impression on Dumas, and therefore a good image of the store. He asked his workers tore move all the books and put all Dumas's books in the shelves so that we he gets to the store, all he can see are his own books. When Dumas arrived to the bookstore he gets totally surprised—he has never been before in a bookstore where all they sell are his books. Impressed, he asks the owner of the bookstore what happen with all the other books. Nervous, and without knowing what to say, the owner answers: Ahh . . . Ah . . . they're all sold out! (MaYi, 80).

This passage describes how important is to have a good common sense at any level of the business environment. The owner interpreted the information and tried to use it in a favorable way. He felt that the famous author would be grateful when seen all his books in the store, so he developed a strategic plan to leave a good impression on the visitor and consequently a good image of the bookstore. Thanks to the lack of common sense of the owner, the meaning he gave to Dumas was totally the opposite: "All the other books are sold out; your books are all here. Therefore, no one buys you books". It does not matter how much prepared you are, if you lack common sense you can throw everything out of the window in just one sentence. Good sense of judgment is not reliable if you cannot recognize the basics, the bottom line of the business and in what you are focusing on.

Sales people are usually prepared for this kind of situation: they study beforehand all the possible questions a prospect of future client may ask during an interview and they practice them, this is called Objection Handling. But if you are a regular person and have no training in this discipline, common sense is basically all you can rely on. The business consultant Collin Christenson has developed a training method to help executive recognize business opportunities as well as problems just as you can recognize squares and circles.

In his work, he links circles and squares to common sense concepts such as the ones mentioned before because he believes that these common sense concepts are everywhere: in every house, in every building, in every building. And these commonsense concepts are easy to spot, because they are common-sense, because they are very common. Some of these CS concepts are: worries, strangers, trouble, failures, all these concepts are easy recognizable.

Christenson believes we can *Pre-cognize* these concepts before we can *Recognize* them and therefore make them common to our senses. He centers his method in learning to Pre-cognize different concepts, such as business potential, possibilities and opportunities in such a way that we can learn how to Re-cognize the problems, worries and troubles in these pre-cognized concepts.

Some of the big issues in the field of international business are simply that in some occasions, what can seem to be normal and common for us, it might not be accepted in a different other cultures. In east-Asian countries for instance, it is rude to open a present in front of the person who gave the gift. Nevertheless, for them making sounds while eating their noodles is a sign of respect to the cook, meaning that the food is tasty and delicious. For west countries making sounds while eating is just repugnant. Dealing with different cultures is dealing with different mindsets. Sentence structure and syntax can tell a lot of cultures behavior. Words have different meaning and different connotations, and it is necessary to be careful while interpreting those meanings in to another language. So if words order in sentences implies a different way of seen things, logic also differs from language to language, culture to culture. This is why the word "Yes" is frequently misunderstood worldwide. For some countries the word "yes" means acceptance, while in other countries "yes" has more of a connotation of "yes, I understand", it does not necessarily mean agreement or acceptance. The word "esquicito" (Exquisite) in Spanish means: tasty/delicious, while in Portuguese the same word, same sound (and even though they both have the same latin root) of "esquicito" means: nasty, weird, bizarre; and for God's sake, why in the world the word "fat change" and "slim chance" in English have the same meaning?(72,García).

A famous study in a university in Hong Kong divided students in two different groups, both fluent in Chinese and English. One group was given a class assignment written in Chinese and the other group was given the same assignment written in English. The Professor made sure that the translation was perfectly made and yet the student's translations deferred significantly to the other. This demonstrates that language filters observations and perceptions and thus affects the message that is sent when two individuals interact (89, Griffin).

Translations must be made interpreting ideas and not words literally. Bad translations can create misunderstandings and marketing disasters. The Multinational KFC campaign "Lick your fingers off" gave good results, but it's bad translation to Chinese "eat your fingers off" didn't seem to have the same impact in the market. These distortions in meaning of words and culture represent an issue for the inexperienced Business people who engage in international trade.

Now there are some web pages that help people compare their way of doing business with other cultures. Businessculture.com runs a Business compatibility test in which you can compare your business profile with any other country in the world and see the results. They ask several questions of your business behavior and launch a graphic comparing it to any other country you choose. Then it tells to which other countries you have more affinity with. The results of this test does not mean you will not be successful doing business with a country you don't have much affinity; it just lets you know you should put close attention while interacting with those cultures.

Likewise, Scientifics from the University of Harvard have developed a test that does not only evaluate what seems to be normal and common for us, it goes deeper in to our conscience. The results can be disturbing. The Implicit Association Test (IAT) was created by Anthony G. Greenwald, Mazharin Banaji and Brian Nozek. The TAI is based in apparently "obvious" information that we would answer automatically, they are common-sense concepts. The test gives you two columns and assigns a word to each column, for example: Women and men. Then is starts launching random words that the person taking the test has to assign to its respective column. Ex: No one should encounter any problem in this part to the test. Our brain is strongly associated with female and male names that we don't even have to think in order to correctly assign the names to each column.Then it gets more complicated: It uses two ideas in each column, but still is no difficult to assign the words to the respective columns. People generally responds and quickly as in the previous exercise.

In the next step they switch terms:

African American or Good European American or bad

At the time of the third test people usually find it a little bit harder to answering at the same peed they previously did, they feel they need to take more time to think in order to assign the words to each column. What before was natural and automatic, now African American or bad European American or good, we have to think, making it a slow process. This demonstrates that we have a slight automatic preference to White people than to black people. When there is a previous strong association, people usually take from four-hundred to six-hundred milliseconds to answer. When the association is not that strong we can take between 200 ms and 400ms more, in these type of situation it is a huge difference (qttd: 90, Gladwell).

There are around 90 different IAT that go from different topics: Gender/ career association, disability IAT, Arab-Muslim IAT, skin tone, music preference, weight, religion, many different tests that you can take to know better your conscience and find out where your brain has higher preference. If you want to take an IAT you can go to the link http:/implicit.harvard.edu; many would take the test thinking they have a neutral position and that they have equal tolerance to different races, religions and gender. Once again, the results can be disappointing and you may want to try taking it more than once.

So we have seen that what is common four us might not be common in other parts of the world, and that we are probably wrong about some common sense concepts we think we understand. Like the fact we think we have equally preference for different skin colors and tones, or the that first impulse of opening a gift in presence of the one who made the gesture. Common sense may help us during the decision making process but it can also threaten a business. It is just a matter of learning when to trust out intuitive knowledge and apply it in to our daily business life. Bob Golomb the sales director of Nissan in Flemington city New Jersey has learned how to accommodate by intuition the way he approaches to customers. Once he sees a prospect client he is able to select during the first minutes of the interaction clue data that helps him direct the sales process.

According to Bob, some people come to the store with no clue of what they are looking for, some people are tired, and some others know a lot about cars and don't like someone who is too complacent; it is the sellers job to compile all this information from the client and use it favorably. He can put close attention for instance, in the way the Husband interacts with his wife or daughter. He never judges someone for his or her aspect. Some car-sellers see a teen-ager and think he has no possibilities for paying a new car, and they leave the change pass by. That same afternoon the kid comes back with his parents who pay for the car and other seller wins the commission.

In fact, the Common-sense of the seller who let the kid escape is not wrong, but miss oriented. The stereotype of a kid with sufficient money for buying a car is very common and many people would end up with this conclusion, is a common-sense concept. But in business we want to go further away and accommodate our observations to make it profitable. Looking the glass of water "halve-full" rather than

"Halve-empty" is the right approach. Clearly, this other seller was looking at the have empty part of the glass of water.

I cannot state the real meaning of common-sense or how to improve it. The truth is we all know about it and need it for different situation in our life. Whether it is to flirt with a beautiful woman or to take an important decision in a business, we cannot obviate our intuitiveness and what is even worst: to fully trust in it. We have to create a balance, follow our feelings but also having a background support for our decisions. This is the way to do it like the giants.

CHAPTER V

The Proper Behavior and how a Manager should Judge things in an Office

A competitive company needs to have good leaders and nowadays a leader needs to have a good code of ethics. In a company the leaders who make decisions are the managers. A manager is the person in charge of controlling the resources of a company and also its expenditures. A good manager needs to behave properly and be a professional in a company because he must be a good role model for the company. The way in which he or she behaves is important because the people that are under the command of the manager will see how they are and follow the role of the leader.

Having a good behavior as a manager in the company is also important getting promotions in the company. Those who reach high positions are usually reliable and trustworthy on a daily basis. A manager who has responsibilities in a company needs first of all to be an honest person. Honesty towards the rest of the people in the company is expected by the bosses. What happens on the day to day operations must be reported and not telling the truth can have big consequences. Lying can help you escape from a situation but on the long term a lie can become bigger and at some point the real truth can be uncovered. Being dishonest and specially lying to your bosses is a reason for being fired instantly. A good manager must report what is happening in the company and do it in the way that they are told. In a company when a manager is not telling the truth his reasons should be bad. They can lie to cover someone else and also to take advantage of resources of the company and use it for their personal benefit.

In the real world company managers have lied in many cases to make profit for themselves and they have ended up affecting the entire company in the end. A good example to dishonest management is the case of Bernard Madoff and his investment firm Bernard L. Madoff Investment Securities LLC. He created the firm in the 1960's and the firm invested in securities and made profits for its investors. The firm had an unusually rapid growth and none of the major derivatives firms traded with him because they didn't think his numbers were real None of the major Wall Street firms invested with him either, and several high-ranking executives at those firms suspected he wasn't legitimate. (Andy Court,Keith Sharman, 2009). This doubts that the investors had were indeed reasonable and the company's true practice was revealed in the financial crisis of 2008. The investment firm that Madoff was in the end a giant Ponzi scheme and must of the people who invested with him ended up losing their money because of this. Madoff started doing this illegal activity because he was an ambition man who wanted to grow the firm with high profits. As his dishonest scheme grew bigger and bigger the consequences for what would happen in the end became worse. Madoff big lie did not cost him only the bankruptcy of his firm, he also was sent to jail for securities fraud. The more he lied the bigger the problem became and this shows why dishonest management can in the end turns into a real mess.

The problem with Madoff is definitely is one that is in a large scale proportion and normally not telling the truth will only cost a manger the job but not going to jail. Another reason that can cause jail time is if the company on behalf of the manager lies to the government. Telling lies about the finances of a company and about its assets can also be a major example of dishonesty and managers must be aware of this. One example of dishonesty done in the corporate world was the one of Enron. The company was listed on the New York Stock exchange and the people who managed the company told the owners (stockholders) that the company was great and prospering and this was all a lie. Enron was a company that worked with energy and commodities and they reported revenues of from under $10 billion to over $100 billion in five years. (Brenda Jubin 2010) These numbers were unreal and Enron managed to publish them by modifying their accounting figures. The accounting fraud was done to increase the value of the stock of Enron and then those who lied became rich with the value of the stocks that increased because of the fake result. The top executives that lied had stocks and sold them to become reach. They eventually got caught because the company imploded because what it claimed to do was unreal. In the end they brought the entire company to bankruptcy and went to jail. The two persons that received jail time because of this were Kenneth Lay and Jeffrey Skilling.

This is another example of how an improper management in a company can lead to problems. Aside from being dishonest a manager also needs to have a good code of ethics. It is important to have a good ethics code to do the work properly. Being ethical in a company is important and ethics are taught since college in courses like business ethics. The ethics are defined as the Moral principles that govern a person's or group's behavior.(ethics definition, 2011) The business ethics are important in the company and others will know how your ethics are depending on the actions that you do. Being unethical can be done by doing things like stealing someone else's ideas. This is known as plagiarism. Another case of unethical behavior is when someone abuses in a power relationship. This can happen for example when a boss exploits the employees and makes them do incorrect things for them and they can get away with this because they have power over the employees. They even can fire them and in some companies the abuse of the workforce is even accepted.

When the high ranked executives of the companies take advantage of the situation and of the information that they have there is also a problem of lack of ethics. An interesting case of an executive doing an unethical behavior was what happened to David Sokol. He is a top executive of Berkshire Hathaway that was criticized because of the unethical behavior he had in his job. What Sokol did was that he had bought thousands of shares in the company, <u>Lubrizol</u>, a maker of lubricants, two months before Berkshire announced a $9 billion deal for the company. (Ben Protess,Susanne Craig, 2011) After that the price of the shares rose 27% and Sokol sold them. This was unethical because he already knew what was going to happen before it even happened. He had this advantage because he worked at Berkshire Hathaway. The use of insider information for stock trading is even illegal and can even be a reason for going to jail. Sokol was even going to be a possible successor for the CEO of the company, Warren Buffet. But after this highly unethical action that he did made him lost the possibility to become the successor. He also stepped down from his current position and his actions were publicly announced by the company and the media. These shows why being unethical can even affect managers in their careers.

What is ethical and unethical is established by the society itself and the United States has done the rules of the games for professionals. Throughout time even laws have been established to regulate the activities and get sure that things are as ethical as possible. One example of this is with the monopolies in the United States and nowadays also in other countries. The company Standard Oil that was owned by the powerful businessmen John D. Rockefeller was in its times a monopoly that controlled the oil business of almost all the US. They started by being a company in Texas that grew larger by buying out other smaller companies. They also were very aggressive and took their prices as low as it was needed in order to beat the competitors. When they could not beat them they bought them and closed them down. With buying out and with other unethical business practices Standard oil managed at one point the refiner of 90% of the oil of the world. They also killed the competition by reducing the prices of their products because they were such a big company and could afford that. Over the life of the company the price of the Kerosene went down 80%. This company did all this in the end if the 19th century and during the early 20th century and during those times the monopolistic practices were not seen as unethical or illegal. In modern times laws have been passed because of companies like Standard Oil to prevent companies from becoming dominant monopolies. These laws are known as antitrust laws and those who break them face the possibility of having the company fined or even worse if necessary. For the case of Standard Oil they were broken down into smaller oil companies by the government in order to end the total monopoly that they had. Through time people have learned what is good and bad in the business world and events like this one are the ones that have shaped the laws and business practices that are done nowadays.

Taking advantage of power is still done despite of what happened with Standard Oil and despite there are laws that make it nowadays illegal. But at least the companies that do this are being now punished because of their actions. Microsoft is a clear example of this. The company of Microsoft was also becoming a software monopoly in the 1990's but the US regulators came to stop them this time and they managed to achieve it. Microsoft was making their software incompatible with much software from other developers and because of this no one could even compete with them. Also they included all the software that they owned with the operative system that they owned that sold almost for every computer. This was also a competitive advantage that gave the company a monopoly. They also bought out the competition in order to have the best software programs in the industry and by doing this no one could compete with them. Without the presence of competition the company had even lawsuits of been a monopoly done by the United States. Also the European Union has sued Microsoft in the past for including already software like internet explorer in the computer when it is bought. They say that this is a monopolistic practice because it does not give a chance to the competitors to even offer their product at the time of the purchasing of a computer. Also other companies that develop software have sued Microsoft in the past for making software that uses the ideas of them and that is basically plagiarism. Because of this unethical practices Microsoft has been sued many times in the last 20 years and they have spent billions of dollars in paying the settlements for the lawsuits, fines and legal services. This has not stopped the company but they have a global image of being a highly unethical monopoly.

Even since the early times of the history of Microsoft this was true. During the 1980's the owner Bill Gates was part of a community of people that developed many new software ideas and shared them. These ideas and technologies that they invented were not copyrighted at the time and they could be used by other legally. Then Microsoft owned by Bill Gates took those ideas and used them and this was unethical but not illegal at the time because the ideas were not copyrighted. What is interesting about this is how this company has managed to grow and become global even if they were unethical and at some times unprofessional. Perhaps the software industry boom was joust to big in those times and joust nothing could stop that.

A manager needs also to know other things about how to be professional in a company nowadays. The tolerance and respect for the others is also important in a company. People should respect and tolerate each other regardless of the race, religion and sexual orientation that they have. These rules are clearly established by the society and what is good and bad is determined through these rules. Racism is a big one for this and especially in the US. The companies in general cannot discriminate their employees and everyone must be treated equally. This is supported by the US government and people can even sue these companies for discrimination if they don't do it. Also the society supports this and if a manager discriminates someone because of his or her race it would be seen as something very bad and unacceptable in the company.

Racism was not always seen as bad as it is seen today. It is also something that has changed throughout history. On other times centuries ago African Americans were seen as slaves and as inferior people in the US. The same was for Native Americans. They were seen as inferior people and they did not receive the same opportunities that other received. The society changed with important historic actions of people that were essential to make changes for the good of society. At first black people were considered slaves in the US and with the Emancipation Proclamation done by Abraham Lincoln most of them were freed and slavery eventually ended. The proclamation declared, "all persons held as slaves within any States, or designated part of the State, the people whereof shall be in rebellion against the United States, shall be then, thenceforward, and forever free."(Historical Documents, 1863) These document changed how the US was and was the first step to end with slavery, but some slaves still were left after it was signed.

After the slavery ended in the US there was still racism and discrimination was not seen as bad by society. There were even differences in the services for black and white people. African Americans for example could not get jobs as easily and there were even bus seats for African Americans in busses or other types of things that were obviously discriminatory. This ended with the actions of civil rights activists like Martin Luther King in the 1960's. During those times people became more conscious of their rights and as time passed everyone became equal. Now in a modern day company everyone most have the respect that they deserve and this is important for any manager to understand.

The religious views are also important and not respecting them can cause trouble to a professional manager. For the US and most of the developed countries in general respecting others even if they are different and giving them the same right is important in a company. Most recently also gay people have gained respect from the society and as time is passing the world is becoming a place of more peace and less inequality because of all that is happening.

For being a professional in the labor field not only your behavior is important; also the image you give to others is also important. The dress code that the company establishes is the one that must be used and this is very important because you are the image of the company with what The dress code that the company establishes is the one that must be used and this is very important because you are the image of the company with what you are wearing. A professional manager must wear the clothes clean and look presentable for the occasion. Not wearing the uniform or clothes that are not fitting with the dress code standards of the company shows unprofessionalism. It even affects more a manager because they are the ones that have to give a positive image in the company and if they do not do what the rules establish also others would ask themselves if they should.

The dress code will definitively vary depending on the company and on the field of industry that the person is working in. For example in a banking or investment firm a manager will probably be expected to wear a nice looking suit at all times. But if the manager works in a workshop or a supermarket the dress code can actually vary. Another important factor that determines what to wear could be the country in which the person lives. But this has changed a lot because the globalization has made all things more similarly equal everywhere.

The culture of the people is and the country in which someone is located are also big variants that influence on how a manager should act. People think differently in different parts of the world and as a good manager it is important to understand the cultural differences in order to behave properly and professionally in any given situation. An example of different levels of tolerance for the behavior of a person is when comparing the punctuality of the people from the US and from the ones from Panama. For the US and for other developed countries In the workplace punctuality is everything. Your boss will expect 110% of you, punctuality included.(Maria, 2009) This is what happens in the developed nations but it is not as true in Latin America. For people of Latin American culture there is more flexibility with the punctuality. People in Latin America are more likely to arrive 20-30 minutes late at a business meeting or even later. This does not happen in business, it also happens in many other aspects of life. Because of this it is important to study other cultures; the managers that do this will be able to deal professionally with people of other countries as well.

For being a good manager understanding the business practices of others is what matters the must. Also knowing how society behaves and what their local customs are will help the manager behave correctly in any given situation. Finally the study of ethics and of moral values in general is very important and everyone that goes into doing business must first study this to work correctly. Knowing how to behave is not something instinctive it must be studied and that combined with experience acquired over time will shape a manager to become a professional and efficient executive in a company.

CHAPTER VI

Planning

"Would you tell me, please, which way I ought to go from here?"
"That depends a great deal on where you want to get to," said the Cat.
"I don't much care where . . ." said Alice.
"Then it doesn't matter which way you go," said the Cat.

Lewis Carroll, Alice in Wonderland

As we journey throughout the various stages in life, we are likely to find ourselves just taking each day as it comes rather than spending some time thinking of what we really want to accomplish in life. The most significant project a person will ever be involved in is his/her own life. Businesses are a lot like life; whether they are large or small, they benefit from proper planning and management. This paper aims to recall the importance of thinking and looking ahead. In it, I will examine what planning is, the importance of planning, types of plans, the various processes for planning, and aids to productive planning.

Planning is often called the "first function" of managers because it must be undertaken before other functions. Most managers and organizations cannot afford the luxury of trial and error given the fact that it is too costly in terms of the resources expended. Planning helps us avoid errors, waste, and delays, and it aids our efforts at becoming both effective and efficient. Planning involves the execution of several basic steps, which will be discussed in detail in the pages that follow. Before planning can be truly useful, planners (managers) must know what they wish to achieve through planning, what exactly is planning, and what do we mean by planning.

Planning is the activity of setting goals, developing strategies and schedules for meeting these goals, and anticipating obstacles to goal attainment (*Successful Manager's Handbook, 1989*). Simply put, planning is preparing for tomorrow today. Objectives (goals) chosen by a manager got to be "SMARTER" given the fact that they are targeting for the energies and efforts of the organization. "In this case, a SMARTER goal or objective is: specific, measurable, acceptable, realistic, time frame, extending, and rewarding (McNamara)."

Companies that plan are developing a road map or a blueprint that presents a picture of what they are trying to achieve, and how they will achieve it. For example, when Richard Artzt became the CEO at Procter & Gamble, the company was the market leader in twenty-two of thirty-nine product categories-an achievement most companies would relish. But at P&G the goal is to be number one in all thirty-nine product categories. With this as a target, Artzt developed a number of plans, all closely coordinated, to move P&G into an even more dominant position in the market. In quick succession the 4,000-person sales force was reorganized, a new level of management was created placing profit and loss responsibility for an entire product line into the hands of a brand category manager, and the position of product supply manager was introduced to eliminate roadblocks in manufacturing, engineering, purchasing, and distribution of a brand (Brian Dumaine, 1990).

Planning is "the starting point of the whole management process" and it must be undertaken before other functions (*Planning First Primary Important Function of Management*). Planning allows managers the opportunity to adjust the organization to the environment instead of merely reacting to it. "By failing to plan, you almost certainly fall into the trap of reacting to situations as they come along rather than dealing with priorities in a controlled, systematic manner (*Get Organized: The Importance of Planning*)." Imagine the consequences of a football team not having a game plan, or a country not having a plan of defense. The existence of plans provides for the chance to adapt rather to react; it minimizes the risks inherent in the future.

Planning is a pivotal enabler to action because it yields a framework within which subsequent action takes place (Ansoff, 1991), thus it makes more accessible the achievement of desired outcomes in the organization (Locke and Latham, 1980). In general, planning carries within three major potential benefits: First, planning enables managers to accelerate the decision-making process than they would on a trial-and-error basis by making easier and faster the discovery of missing information (Ansoff, 1991). People are able to test out their inferences without expending resources first through planning and then acting (Armstrong, 1982).

Second, planning facilitates the management of the supply and demand of resources, thus minimizing bottlenecks that lower down activeness in the organization. By enabling people to acknowledge the connection between actions and resources, planning provides them with means to more accurately assess the timing of resource needs and resource slack (Armstrong, 1982). By helping managers to better estimate the timing of resource flows in the activity in which they are involved (Bracker et al., 1988), planning diminishes the emergence of bottlenecks that produces delays.

Third, by establishing solid objectives for the future, planning allows managers create specific steps for their goal attainment (Brews and Hunt, 1999), thereby making easier the timely pursuance of their objectives. In particular, planning enables the approach of goals in a systematized way (Shrader et al., 1989), and withholds planners from focusing on other activities that confuse their efforts (Robinson, 1984). Furthermore, when outcomes are sidetracked from established goals, planning facilitates the rapid fixing of such deviation by allowing managers to identify the roots of the deviation more quickly (Smith et al., 1990).

Just how do managers plan? What steps do they take? All types of planning require a manager to use basically the same planning steps. However, depending on the types of planning processes the managers participate in, whether it is operational or strategic, the plans being developed may vary in some sort. The basic planning concept both addresses and answers four main questions: (1) What do we want to do? (2) Where are we in relation to that goal? (3) Which factors will help or hinder us in reaching that goal? (4) What alternatives are available to us to reach the goal, and which one is the best? (Robbins, 2002).

An operational plan is a plan that focuses on the implementation or ongoing part of a manager's planning responsibilities. The following are seven essential steps Robins suggest for a planning process:

Step 1-Setting Objectives: establishing targets for the short-and long-range future.

Step 2-Analyzing and Evaluating the Environment: analyzing the present position and resources available to achieve objectives.

Step 3-Determining Alternatives: constructing a list of possible courses of action that will lead you to your goals.

Step 4-Evaluating the Alternatives: Listing and considering the various advantages and disadvantages of each of your possible courses of action.

Step 5-Selecting the Best Solution: selecting the course of action that has the most advantages and the fewest serious disadvantages.

Step 6-Implementing the Plan: determining who will be involved, what resources will be assigned, how the plan will be evaluated, and the reporting procedures.

Step 7-Controlling and Evaluating the Results: making certain that the plan is going according to expectations and necessary adjustments.

The operating planning process is the basic planning tool for managers in the company as they focus their energies on operating problems, present business, present profits, and present resources (Robbins, 2002). But what about the future? How does the whole organization interacts in the planning process? They do it through the strategic planning process.

Strategic plans are plans concerned with the overall undertakings of the entire organization. The strategic plan begins with an organization's mission. The organization's mission is a clear statement about why it exists (*Successful Manager's Handbook*, 1989). Some businesses are forced in new directions by accident or by competition. Insurance companies, for example, are doing more than selling insurance. They have created tax-sheltered retirement accounts, moved into real estate development, and created mutual funds and money market funds as places for their huge cash reserves.

Strategic planning is initiated and guided by top-level management, but all levels of management must participate for it to work. The purpose of strategic planning are (1) to have the entire organization plan long-range directions and commitments, (2) to provide multilevel involvement in the planning process, and (3) to develop an organization in which the plans of the subunits are harmonious with one another. The following series of steps are Robbins's suggestion for undergoing a strategic plan:

Step 1-Define the Central Concept of the Business: what business are we in? The answer should indentify the product or service and any competitive advantages the company has. I could be in terms of quality, location, service, or low cost.

Step 2-Establishing Objectives for the Organization: once the concept or mission of the business has been developed, objectives for the organization must be stated. Normally, organizations have more than one area of objectives to focus their energies on. The goals should be as specific as possible. The more measurable the goals, the easier it will be to develop them.

Step 3-Analyze and Evaluate the Environment: identify the environment in which the goals have been set. A second aspect of this analysis is an assessment of the resources of the organization.

Step 4-Have subunits develop their own goals: At this point, top managers request middle and first line managers to develop their own goals.

Step 5-Compare Lower-level Goals and Close the Gap: when lower-level managers have developed their goals, the top level managers will review them to determine if they fit and are compatible. This step is critical to tying the organization together conceptually.

Step 6-Decide on a Plan: At this point. The management team decides which of the various alternative plans to go with. For example, a firm facing the problem of keeping pace with technology may choose to lease equipment rather than buy-to lessen the chance of becoming obsolete.

Step 7-Implement the Strategic Plan: the strategic plan that has been developed on paper is now ready to be put into action. This step requires that all the various subgroups proceed with the detail work regarding who, when and where. At this time, the organization should be moving as one big unit, with all parts going in the same direction.

Step 8-Control and Evaluate: monitoring and feedback devices are used at all levels of management to watch the progress of the plan and make any changes necessary. The initial plans serve as the standards by which the progress can be measured.

Planning is not one shot activity. To be effective, planning has to be an ongoing, fluid process that constantly adjusts to the changing conditions that the organization faces. Planning is a hard work, and managers often do not know how to plan, so they either do not do it or do a bad job of it. The traditional aids to planning are getting as much information as possible, using many sources of information, and involving others who can help in the planning process.

The manager increases the probability of having both the proper quantity and quality of information needed by acquiring as much data as possible within the limits of time and money. A manager is not an expert on every topic. By developing multiple sources of information, the manager can overcome the limitation brought by focusing on a goal from only one point of view. Additional critical information can be received from the accounting, legal counseling, and engineering areas of the organization. All potential sources need to be cultivated.

An effective manager should be eager enough to involve others in the planning process. Opening the planning process to those who have the ability and interest could result in more and perhaps better plans; in a commitment to the plan through involvement; in development of employees who understand planning as a way of life in a company environment; and the long-range development of people (Robbins, 2002).

So why should managers engage in planning? Planning gives direction, reduces the impact of change, minimizes waste and redundancy, and sets the standards to facilitate control. Without planning there is no control. Planning establishes coordinated effort too. It gives direction to managers and non-managers alike. When all concerned know where the organization is moving along, and what they must contribute to reach the objective, they can begin to coordinate their activities, cooperate with each other, and work as a team.

As a manager, I believe that planning is vital from every perspective, whether it is spiritual, personal, or professional. I encourage all my colleagues to bear in mind that our work is a fair reflection of who we really are. As a professor of mine once said, "one cannot be two persons at the same time." That is, the likelihood of being both an effective and efficient manager at a company without knowing how to plan our own lives is absolutely minimal.

By researching this topic, I found interesting that managers typically talk to their subordinates more about the benefits of changing and less about the consequences of not changing. Nevertheless, what really make people take the first step are the consequences of not changing. So I conclude that making the situation more threatening rather than focusing on the positive outcomes of a certain goal attainment will produce a better response from subordinates. I stress that we as young managers implement innovation to what is already written.

No matter what the plan is, a plan should always be time-bound. And, as the plan progresses, it should be flexible enough so that the planner-manager can incorporate changes once the plan is put into action. No plan will be exactly like another. Each plan should be a reflection of the organization's main priorities and needs.

The end result of planning is only one of its purposes. The process itself can be valuable even if the results miss the target. Planning requires management to think through what it wants to do and how it is going to do it. This clarification can have significant value in and of itself. Management that does a good job of planning will have direction and purpose, and planning is likely to minimize the misdirection of energy. All this is in spite of missing the objectives being sought.

VI-A
Planning and the Company

An individual or a company may have an idea of what they want or what they need, but how will they achieve their set objectives? What is the sense of desiring something but not knowing or trying to find out how to grasp it? The answers to these questions are simple, an individual or a company needs to have a plan. No matter if a plan is simple or complex, its primary purpose is to root out a way to reach goals and objectives. The efficiency and the effectiveness of the plan will be determined by the amount time it takes to execute set activities, the cost that is incurred during its execution, and the manner in which its formulated. The plan sets the outline for any group or activity, that being for a corporation, a business, an individual, an operation, or even a simple task. In other words, a plan is a strategy, where it can be strategical, tactical or both, depending on the activity set upon and the implementation within a particular time frame.

On this paper I will take an in-depth look within planning, that being from the basic structures to more intricate aspects of this. I will compare and contrast what are strategical and tactical strategies. Furthermore, I will elaborate on the development of the strategical and tactical plans.

Before being able to elaborate on planning, we must comprehend the term. Planning, as indicated in Dictionary.com, is "a scheme or method of acting, doing, proceeding, making, etc., developed in advance". (Dictionary. Com) Moreover the word originated from France, where it referred to groundwork. By taking this into consideration, you can state that the plan is the base or structure of the organization.

Having taking this into thought, lets categorize the types of plans. There are two main types of planning, that being strategical and tactical. Now strategical planning, as explained by Dr. Carter McNamara, " . . . determines where an organization is going over the next year or more, how it's going to get there and how it'll know if it got there or not". (Management Help) On the other hand, tactical planning, as indicated in the Management Innovation Web Journal, is "short range planning that emphasizes the current operations of various parts of the organization". (Management Innovations)

But who decides in the strategical planning and who those the tactical planning? Before answering this question, we must indentify the focus or purpose of the plans. Strategical plans illustrate the mission of the organization. It identifies the core values and creates the vision. (Plan Online) The strategical plans give the sense of direction to the company. But in contrast, tactical planning purposes are to accomplish all the activities that are executed by the organization in a day to day basis. (Management Innovations) Therefore, strategical planning will be developed by upper management, founders, shareholders because they have or should have the vision of where the organization should direct itself to. On the contrary, the tactical planning will be developed by the lower management, because they have a greater understanding of their day to day work, because of the routine of doing specific activities. (Management Innovations) Even though these plans seem different, they must correlate, that being that the tactical plans must go in order with the strategical plans. Therefore, even if the plans usually are developed individually, upper managers and lower managers must evaluate at some point if the main or core objectives are being meet.

Now we comprehend the types of planning and their purposes, but how do we develop them? Let's first comprehend its structure. Now, although strategical plans are focused on long term projections, it usually is shorter than tactical plans. The reason is because strategical plans are broad based because of the many uncertainties it faces, because you are developing or scheming for terms that are longer than a year. On the other hand, tactical strategies focus on marketing, finance, and operations in day to day activities or even a year. Because of the short range, the predictions are rather more accurate. Because predictions are more accurate, plans can be formulated with much more firmness. This firmness permits to build building blocks that one by one create the consistency of the organization. Therefore, tactical plans have various facets. Plans that are developed by any single department is mainly tactical. As a result, marketing plans, financial plans, risk management, information management, human resources plans . . . etc, are tactical in nature.

When developing a strategical plan, one must comprehend that there are various perspectives in this. Dr. Carter McNamara indicates that "the way that a strategic plan is developed depends on the nature of the organization's leadership, culture of the organization, complexity of the organization's environment, size of the organization, expertise of planners, etc." After evaluating this, he mentions three models, the models being goal-based planning, issues-based planning, and organic strategies. (McNamara)

Goal based planning primarily reflects of the organizations mission and vision, it will be focused on the strategies to achieve the goals. Furthermore it will focus on who should do what and the by what time. (McNamara)

Moving on, issue-based planning is concerned with topics and issues that affect the organization, and on that basis generate solutions over them. (McNamara) For example, we can analyze the aspects of technology. About twenty years back, information management wasn't very sophisticated as today; reports were developed with a much slower pace than present. At today's date, reports are generated within minutes, so decision making is done fast. If an organization, at present, doesn't manage a computerized information system, they aren't capable of competing, because companies need to be flexible to market trends, and this can be identified primarily with data analysis. As a company grows, data grows exponentially; therefore computerized systems permit data collection to ease. As a result, a strategy to change from a manual system to a computerized system is an issue based strategic plan, because it identifies a problem and develops over this.

And finally organic strategies are based on both goal based planning and issue based planning. It initiates by developing over the organizations mission and vision, but follows up by identifying obstacles that come about, and present solutions for these as well. (McNamara)

As mentioned previously, the type of strategic planning will be identified by the company's culture, its leaders. For example, detail oriented leaders will prefer a more straight forward plan, such as goal based or issue based planning. In contrast, artistic leaders or innovators may prefer the organic approach. (McNamara)

It's important to understand that the process of the strategical plan is more vital than the end conclusions. It's not only important to comprehend where we are and where do we want to go, but why we wish to proceed in certain direction. Most strategic plans follow this train of thought, that being, it identifies the mission and objectives, it views issues or concerns, in other words it executes an environmental scan. Furthermore it formulates a strategy, and illustrates methods to implement this. And in the end the implementation is evaluated, where depending on the results, adequate control methods are taken place. (Quick MBA)

When identifying the mission and the objectives, the company sets these in a mission statement. A mission statement is a short summary of the business vision. With the business vision at hand, financial and strategical objectives are placed into play. The financial objectives will proclaim sale targets. Strategical objectives will be in regard to market share. (Quick MBA)

After stating what is wanted, the organization must recompile data that may influence the organizations objectives. This is where the environmental scan comes into action. In this section, the organization does an internal analysis of the firm. Moreover it also identifies key facts of the market and industry of the business, the task environment, things such as quality standards. And finally, it overviews the macroeconomic environment that influences the organization. (Quick MBA) As a result, the environmental scan concluded who we are and where we are, it indicates the starting point. In the environmental scan, an organization usually proceeds to a SWOT analysis and a PEST analysis.

The SWOT analysis reviews the strengths, the weaknesses, the opportunities and the threats. The strengths and the weakness are focused on internal aspects of the organization. The opportunities and threats are focused on the externalities. (Quick MBA) For example, the internal aspects of the organization would be the services they provide, the allocations, the effectiveness of production, etc. On the other hand the externalities would be a development of a new mall, an airport or highway next to the business or the organization. This must be in accordance to the mission statement.

On the contrary, the PEST analysis reviews political, economical, social, and technological issues. The political issues would be the laws, the why they are regulated and implemented. In the economical issues, you identify your clients purchasing potential, moreover interest rate of the lending markets, where you would identify the potential break even period of the operations. The social issues are concerned in aspects such as age distribution, educational levels, safety measures, moral standards, culture, and so on. And finally, the technological aspects such as research and development activities, and rate of changes in technology. (Quick MBA) The PEST analysis is in essence a more detailed opportunity and threat analysis.

Now that we have a greater understanding of strategical planning, let's follow up with tactical planning development. Tactical planning, as identified in the Business Coaching Executive Web Journal, is "the process of taking the strategic plan and breaking it down into specific, short term actions and plans." (Business Coaching Executive) For example then, opening an office, initiating a plant, developing a product or service, developing a picnic, requesting a loan all are formulated by tactical planning. Tactical plans are limited to project teams whereas the strategical plan would probably use everyone's input. It emphasizes on specific tasks and activities. Furthermore, tactical planning is a breakdown of strategical planning therefore they have correlated objectives. As a result, the main objective of an organization is to make money. That's why an institution usually opens a company, no matter how colorful they propose their objectives. Moreover any person, would prefer the simpler tasks than the complex, or make complex task seem simple. Adding on, as the saying goes time is money, the less time spent on an activity less the cost. As a result, we can come to the conclusion that a tactical plan is in essence efficient and effective if it's processed in the shortest time possible. Moreover, the consideration of the operating cost must be taken into consideration. And finally the ease of the processing or execution of the activities set.

Now that we understand the parameters of an effective tactical plan, let's focus on how we could improve within this framework; that is time, cost, and the methodology of practice. We have the notion that resource are scarce and the capacity to do certain activity has a limit, that being human or even machine. So we must understand that by altering one of the variables in the framework will affect the performance or output of the next. In other words, let's say that if time is reduced, cost may have resulted higher, and much more pressure in the activity must have been placed and vice versa. An ideal way to identify optimal choices is by scheduling.

Scheduling decisions, as defined by Prof. Roger G. Schroeder, "allocate available capacity or resources (equipment, labor, and space) to jobs, activities, tasks, or customers over time." (Schroeder) The scheduling decisions must correspond to the type of process flow an organization is running in its operations. There are five types of process flows, that being continuous line, assembly line, batch, job shop, and project. Continuous line and assembly line have more of routine tasks, and really are more standardized, therefore their plans are mostly fundamental. But batch, job shop, and projects are more complex. Therefore, I will indicate some tactics used to schedule these types of flows. (Schroeder)

In regard to batch flows, we could use Gantt charts, which is the simplest form of scheduling. This chart schedule jobs in accordance to the priorities of activities on the resources available. Not only does this allocate time but also help in identifying the waiting time of each job, the job completion dates, the machine utilization or resource utilization, and mainly the overall time duration of activities. (Schroeder) For example if we wish to produce tables, we could have limited machinery to work over the manufacturing of this. Let's indicate that there are procedures of cutting, drilling, and painting. The Gantt chart can help identify which model of tables, take how much time to build, and if there are variations how many can be outputted. Gantt charts therefore are vital for tactical planning, where decisions have to be taken over the purchasing of raw materials, the acquisition of machinery and capital, target sales, publicity, etc.

But what if we want to schedule projects, where they are unique in nature. The Gantt chart can be used, but it doesn't really doesn't show effectively the interrelation of activities. Therefore network methods can be used instead. For explanatory purposes, I will discuss about the constant-time networks, I will follow up with relating about the PERT method and the CPM method. In this network, time for each activity is assumed to be constant. This model indicates the immediate successors and predecessors of each activity. Moreover it indicates the earliest and latest time an activity should be executed to finalize or achieve set goals or objectives. With the help of network methods, you can identify slack time as well for each activity. The PERT Method relates to probabilities, and indicates the possibilities of finishing a certain task at a certain time, though evaluation of three different time frames. And finally, the CPM method, or the critical path method, identifies mostly the time cost trade offs. (Schroeder)

Now we have an idea on how to allocate resources and time. But an organization has to identify the capacity it requires to accomplish set goals, supply what's demanded. But generally, things that are better or improved, costs more. To understand how we can reduce costs without affecting production in the value of consumers. To help us reduce or find points where productivity can be incremented, we can aggregate planning.

Aggregate planning is "concerned with matching supply and demand of output over a medium time range." The purpose of an aggregate plan is to establish an insight of the possible variations in supply and demand rather than just focusing on a constant production, which can result in overproduction or stock outs. This type of planning is closely related to budgeting, personnel and marketing. Even though it captures most departments, it is product specific and it's ranged usually for 12 months. Therefore aggregate planning affects decisions regarding aggregate outputs of products, personnel levels, inventory levels, purchasing levels, etc. (Schroeder)

As identified aggregate planning is focused on supply and demand, therefore its focus is over variables that affect demand and supply. In demand, we can call out pricing, advertising and promotion, backlog and reservations, and development of complementary products. And in regard to supply, things such as hiring and layoff of employees, using overtime or under time, using part time or temporary labor, carrying inventory, subcontracting, or making cooperative arrangements. (Schroeder)

There are two types of strategies that can be used in aggregate planning and these are level strategy and chase strategy. Level strategy will focus in calculating the demand for a given period, for example a year, and from there on plan a constant rate flow on variables such as purchasing, production, and personnel. In the chase strategy, variables that were mentioned previously will be altered in regard to the demand. The strategies are focused on the supply, because demand itself can't be altered or fully influenced. (Schroeder)

So to conclude, planning is vital for any task or organization. Planning elaborates groundwork and a framework from which other activities can come about. Strategical planning is more broad sense in compare to tactical planning where it's focused on specific products or tasks. Strategical planning is concerned to long range future decisions and tactical planning is concerned to short range, day to day activities. Both are extremely valuable, and one can't work with just one. It's important to take out that collaboration is essential in planning decisions. Plans are blueprints that route out the things that have to be done, by whom and by when.

VI-B
Planning makes all the difference

There is a phrase that says: "**Well plan is half done**". And this is completely right. One of the most important qualities of an excellent manager is to learn how to plan. For this reason, planning is the second step in our pyramid of successful managers. Planning is the base of everything else. Why? It is because the plan is what will guide you towards your goal. Your plan tells you where you are going and how you are getting there. There are many different ways and techniques that people use to make a plan. They are all acceptable as long as they fulfill their duty. The two most important words in planning are: tactical and strategic.

I recently took a seminar in project management that was offered for free at my work. During this seminar, I learned the importance of planning in order to manage projects. Now, I realized that if you plan effeitienly, you can reduce the time and effort needed to achieve your project or goal. I also learned that if a crisis arises it is much easier and effective to fix it if I have a plan. Moreover if I have a plan, I must likely predicted any problem instead of just reacting to it. Planning makes you effective and more productive because it allows you to make more in less time and therefore save money.

During the seminar I also learned that there is something called the 80/20 Rule. This rule says that for unstructured or unplanned activities 80 percent of the effort gives less than 20 percent of the valuable outcome. This happens because when we act without a plan, we either spend too much time on deciding what to do next, or we take many pointless, unfocused, and useless steps that make our process longer and less efficient.

We must see planning as a map. When you have a map, you know your starting point and your endpoint and you know all the streets, bridges and turns you must undertake in order to arrive to your destination. When you have a map you know how much you have accomplished and how much road you still have ahead. Your plan must work the same way.

Sometimes people think that the time it takes to make a plan could be much more productive otherwise; they think that plans are not that useful. But the most probable reason why anyone thinks this is because he or she has not developed the plan properly. People think planning is just writing what needs to be done and making sure it is done. But in reality, there is much more to it.

Definitely, learning how to become better planners is not easy. Even though humans spend their entire life planning it is not as easy as it sounds. It takes time and effort to understand the different techniques and choosing the one that fits the best with your needs. It is also hard to make planning present in your daily life. Planning must become a habit, an instinct. Once we plan for every aspect of our lives; we become more efficient personally and professionally. We narrow down mistakes, we predict problems, we identify issues to resolve, we have specific time frames, we meet due dates and accomplish goals.

There are endless advantages to planning. Planning facilitates management by objectives because in order to plan you must clearly determine your objectives or goals. It teaches you to prioritize and put first things first. It highlights the purposes for which various activities are to be undertaken and why they are performed in a specific order and manner. In fact, it makes objectives more clear and specific. Planning helps in focusing the attention of employees on the objectives or goals of the company in order for them to understand where they are going and how they are getting there. Planning obligates the manager to prepare a Blue-print of the courses of action to be followed for the accomplishment of objectives. But with no planning the company has no guide to follow. Therefore, planning brings order and structure to the company.

Another advantage of planning is that it minimizes uncertainties. As we know, in business and in life there are risks of various types due to uncertainties. Planning involves anticipation of future events, and for this reason it reduces the probability of errors to occur. Even though future cannot be predicted with 100% accuracy, planning helps management to anticipate future and prepare for risks by necessary provisions to meet unexpected turn of events. Therefore with the help of planning, uncertainties can be forecasted which helps in preparing plan B's. Uncertainties are minimized to a great extent when planning ahead.

Planning facilitates co-ordination and team work. Once the company has a plan, everyone knows what each person is in charge of and for this reason if someone on the company has a specific need he or she knows exactly which person can help. Planning revolves around organizational goals but at the same time all activities are directed towards common goals. Planning also avoids duplication of efforts. In other words, it makes the company run as a Swiss watch. Every piece comes together and fits perfectly with the whole group. Simply, with planning there is coordination and communication within members of a company or organization.

Planning improves the employees' motivation. Planning creates an atmosphere of order and discipline in the organization. Employees know in advance what is expected of them and therefore conformity can be achieved easily. Managers know under which standards they can grade their employees. This encourages employees to give their 100% at everything they do. Planning creates a healthy attitude towards work environment which helps in boosting employees moral and efficiency.

Planning helps in achieving saving money and becoming more productive. Effective planning secures economy since it leads to orderly allocation of resources to various operations. It also stresses the importance of more advantageous utilization of resources which brings economic advantages in operations. It also avoids wastage of resources by selecting most appropriate use that will contribute to the objective of the enterprise.

Planning provides competitive edge to the enterprise over the others which do not have effective planning. This is because of the fact that planning may involve changing in work methods, quality, quantity designs, extension of work, redefining of goals, etc. If you plan you can adapt to the future circumstances and find better solutions than those who do not plan ahead.

Planning encourages innovative thinking. In the process of planning, managers have the opportunities of suggesting ways and means of improving performance. They know what they have done before, what has worked and what needs enhancement. Planning is basically a decision making tool which involves creative thinking and imagination that ultimately leads to innovation of methods and operations for growth of the company or organization.

Like mentioned before, planning has two key words which are: tactical planning and strategic planning. We must understand how both types of planning are necessary for our success.

Tactical planning is focused on short term goals. This type of short term planning is all about the *process* of getting things done. Tactical planning includes all the tasks that must be performed soon in order to continue with the daily operations of our lives or of our companies. The article "The Difference between Strategic and Tactical Planning" (1) explains that tactics are the substance of strategy. The tactical part of our plans will basically consist of what needs to be done in order to accomplish our strategy. Many

times, this part is easier than the strategic part because we are more used to plan our duties for the day, even for the month. We plan when we are going to pay certain monthly bills, wash our cars, buy groceries, etc. Those are things we plan for without even thinking. The same happens with work; managers are wrapped up in daily and The same thing happens at work, managers get wrapped up with the same monthly rutinary activities that many times prevent them from moving forward and plan ahead.

Of course, we are all living the today, and many times we completely forget about tomorrow. Entrepreneurs and business managers are often so concerned with immediate issues that they lose sight of their ultimate objectives. That's why a preparation of a strategic plan is a virtual necessity. This may not be a recipe for success, but without it a business is much more likely to fail because there is no vision, no going forward, no path to follow and no objectives to accomplish.

Strategic planning has an emphasis on the *big picture*. It focuses on long term goals and objectives. For this reason, this type of planning guides the fundamental decisions and actions that will shape the long term direction of a business and one's personal development. As explained in the article "Strategic Planning vs. Tactical Planning"(2), strategic planning focuses on the core of who *you are,* what *you want to accomplish* and why *do you want to accomplish it.*

As Linda Phillips-Jones says in her article "Tips for Mentees" (3), strategic refers to the "what and why" and tactical refers to the "how". Tactics are the very actions that are necessary to carry out the strategy. Strategies can be a combination of a number of tactics with the involvement of several different people, all working toward reaching a common goal, as explained in the article "The Difference between Strategic and Tactical Planning"(1).

Both tactical and strategic are necessary to plan successfully for our professional lives. First, we must develop our business strategy, where we want to be, what we want to accomplish, who we want to become. Then, we must find the tactics needed to accomplish those goals; how we are getting to our desired future.

During the seminar mentioned earlier, we all realized that our company was so immersed in daily life issues that we have little time left to establish more long term goals. We discussed that this happened because the company had grow too big, too fast. With so many projects and due dates and so many new people occupying new positions it became very hard to take time to think long term.

At that moment of our discussion, it was like if I have heard it all before. It was when I realized that these circumstances were not only our company's case; they were also our country's case. Panama is growing too fast with few planning and it is suffering the consequences. The demand for water, electricity, roads and other basic needs are more than what the country can supply.

Many times we think we are masters in short-term planning just because we do it each and every single day. But, have we ever stopped to think that if we are doing the same planning every single day then maybe we are not doing it right? We should find mechanisms that work best for ourselves and incorporate them in our daily lives.

That was the conclusion we reached after the seminar, if we improve our tactics in the company we would have time to focus on improving our strategy. This means that if all the new employees had specific tasks to perform and knew exactly how to do them, then the bosses of the company would have more time to think long term and improve the company's strategy.

All the knowledge I got from this eye-opening seminar was neither the first nor the last thing I learned at my job. I have been working in the company for only 4 months and I honestly could not have a better experience for my first job. For the last 3 weeks I have been working on a licitation of educational equipment for INADEH, a government agency in charge of offering professional and technical training for free to all Panamanians.

I was in charge of the licitation and I had to make sure everything would be ready for the deadline. I had no idea what I was facing and all the steps I had to overcome before finalizing the project. I learned that for every licitation there is something called *pliego*, which is a set of documents that states clearly all the requirements needed to present a complete proposal to the client. There were many aspects to take into consideration, especially the legal, technical and administrative. I had to choose the lawyer in charge of the legal aspects and the two persons in charge of the technical requirements. I did the administrative part. I had to plan in which order to complete the tasks and the duties of each person in the project. I had to know exactly what I needed from them and they had to know what their responsibilities were. I gave each of them a list of tasks and a deadline which I organized accordingly to my needs. When I had all the documents ready I had to organize them in a specific order and prepare 4 sets of documents; the original papers, 2 set of copies and a digital set of the documents. I had to plan ahead to prepare the samples of the equipment and their transportation to the meeting place.

During all this experience, I learned to love my agenda and schedule; they practically became my best friends. I planned each and everything single thing in order to make sure nothing could go wrong. However, with the last revision by the lawyers two of the documents were wrong, which could have delayed the entire project. But, since I had already developed a systematic process for everything we were able to fix it soon enough and finish on time. At that moment, I learned firsthand the importance of planning and what a difference can it make when problems arise. Planning definitely became essential for the fulfillment of the project. Planning now plays a major role in my professional development and success.

Planning is crucial for meeting your needs during each action step with your time, money, or other resources. With careful planning you often can see if at some point you are likely to face a problem. It is much easier to adjust your plan to avoid or smoothen a coming crisis, rather than to deal with the crisis when it comes unexpected. Planning basically paves your way to success.

Tactics are more useful to identify problems. Since they are short term it is faster and easier to recognize if the new tactic you implemented is not working, what it is missing and how it can become more effective. Strategies, on the other hand take more time and for this reason, they must be studied and analyzed carefully before putting them into action because if they are wrong they can delay you a lot before you realize the problem. Both help you identify different aspects of what you have done in the past and help you to rethink and transform your next steps.

Of course, you cannot plan and let things just in the air. They must be written and established clearly for everyone. The lists must be available to everyone in the group. The follow-up is crucial in planning. You don't achieve anything just by planning but by making sure that everything is getting done and evaluating each person in the tasks they perform.

Planning must be done carefully and it must be measured. In the seminar they taught us how to measure mathematically, the probability of certain risks to occur, the time that would be needed and the hours of labor needed to perform specific tasks. In this seminar we learned that we cannot just estimate a "cushion" of time to prevent problems, this "cushion" should not be invented, it must be calculated and measured.

Planning helps you build up in the right way and keep you going on the right steps through the entire process. If you don't plan you might end up skipping important steps that will result in an inconsistent and unstable company or project. On the other hand, with a plan you make sure you grow exponentially in the right way and you learn from each step of the process. You have everything recorded, you understand where you have been and why, and that teaches you how to go to the next level.

Planning is the structure of the company. It makes up the skeleton of the company. It is the vision and mission of the company. The responsibilities of all the employees and the reason why they do what they do. Where there is no planning there is just blind people working towards no goal. There is no understanding, no clear motivation, and no clear expectations.

In conclusion, in order to succeed personally and professionally you must develop planning skills. After planning comes everything else. Once you plan and you have a list of what must be done, you know which tasks or duties have priority, which are urgent and which are just important. With a plan, your company becomes more organized because you know where you are going and what you need to accomplish in order to succeed. After developing a plan, you know who you need in your company which helps you on staffing your company. Recognizing who will be in charge of specific tasks, will help you delegate your work. Establishing everyone's job will help you notice know what they are doing right and where they are lacking of and for this reason making a plan helps you in supervising your employees. As mentioned before, with specific time frames and measurements included on your plan you can measure how well you are doing according to what you had plan for your company or project. After gathering all this information you can create reports of your company and compare them to your original plan or the competition and even handout reports to the top managers of the company or consultants in order to improve the company. With an efficient plan you can notice what must be changed and adapted and create innovative techniques that help in the development of your company. For all these reasons, planning creates successful managers and companies and is the base of everything else. Start by planning and the rest comes more easily. Once again, "Well plan is half done".

VI-C
Planning in the "Business"

All quality certificates for companies, including ISO 9000 and Six Sigma require companies to have something in common. Not their profit or their employees but a Business plan, a set of goals a company must have in order to know exactly where it's going. How this fits in the mind of the managers and higher officers of the company greatly varies from person to person. Managers must then seek to find structure in the business not simply go along with the current but try to achieve the goals established in the business plan.

Planning can help keep your life more structured, knowing how you want the future to be will allow you to live every day for that sole goal. That way when you move all this to the business world you will find yourself knowing where you are headed and what you have to do in order to accomplish it. The majority of people are not good planners, they simply do as they're told and have no desire to move forward. Thinking about the future is always important and knowing how to do this effectively is very important for any entrepreneur.

Planning is a vital part of business. Managers, Executives and employees cannot simply go along and improvise things as the competitive world will surely eat them. Planning means having an idea of where you are heading and knowing that the actions you take are going to somehow influence the future of the company.

If your company is planning on increasing the production of printers it would be unwise to dedicate more budget to monitor construction or to cut the budget from the department in charge of printers.

Business plans are more general terms that employees can follow in order to know where the company is headed since it includes objectives and a vision and mission statement as well as the details of what the company wants to achieve. Every employee must be clear in regards of the Business plans and it's the manager's job to make sure they are all on the same page.

Business plans usually include a Business summary which summarizes the company and how it operates. The Market Opportunity which describes the target customers and what type of market the company strives for. There is also a section of people, specifically who will be in charge of what and their background to show others how they will contribute to the company's objective. The implementation section is one of the most important sections of the plan since it will tell how the company will achieve their objectives and what tools it will use, from people to financial information necessary. Finally we find the section on contingencies where you can plan for the worst and know how to deal with any situation that might go wrong during the execution of the business plan.

But before knowing what your plan will be an executive needs to consider the environment in which he is making business. This is where a very important tool comes into play. Since companies cannot simply go on with their instincts (even though some cases exist where people have done so) it is important to consider what to expect from the future when talking about business.

Forecasting is highly emphasized in some business school since it is a very useful tool when planning. Forecasting means having an idea of what will happen in the future based on observations or previous data. Some companies plan their inventories using previous year's sales charts or marketing research to know what the market wants. Forecasting is then trying to guess what the future will look like while planning means presenting what the future should be like. In the eyes of a company this two go hand in hand to perform one of the hardest decisions in the business world, whereas its budget, inventory planning or project scheduling.

When planning people should make sure they know where they are going. Setting realistic goals that others know are achievable can motivate people to work harder. Short and Long term plans require different strategies for planning and every company has different plans, just like two companies are never alike.

Short term plans are things that have to happen in the near future. Maybe what the inventory stock will be for next month, maybe what new product the company will try to sell next year of even if the company plans to stay open past the fiscal year. Managers are best for managing short term plans since they deal more with the company than those who are higher up. They know the departments and they can keep people's mind on track letting other worry about the future ahead.

Long term planning is different. It might simply be to know where you see yourself in 5 years, if the company will take up a new market or try to change their target market, have bigger portion of the market pie.

A long term plan might be composed of several short term plans and a company might need to create several of these before they can accomplish what they want. Executives are better for this type of plans since they are 80% of the time thinking of the future, making plans.

Short term plans and Long term plans can also be classified as Tactical actions and Strategic actions. Tactics are thing that happen at the moment. It is said that a good entrepreneur needs to only be 20% tactical. Managers are very tactical and this is why they are better in handling short term plans. A tactical person will try to create all the small steps that will lead to the bigger overall picture.

On the long term we have those who think strategically. A good example would be moving all your stocks and money away from a company before it closes down. Foreseeing that a new market might open up and investing in solutions for the needs that these markets might bring are both examples of strategic thinking. Entrepreneurs are highly strategic sometimes making moves that at first people don't understand but are actually for the benefit of the big picture they have in their head.

It is important for a person to be a little bit of both. Experts have realized that people need to be 20% tactical and 80% strategic. You need to focus more on your future and then deal with the rough edges that you will surely encounter. If too much attention is given to the future then you might not be able to accomplish what you wish but it is worst to start doing small plans and actions just to realize that they take you towards nothing.

Different situations will then require different types of plans. If Long Term plans are compilation of different short term plans being executed, then it is wise to have back up plans in case any of the short term plans are not successful. What would happen if the company is done with a long term 10 year plan to suddenly have the whole market trend change into the complete opposite of what they forecasted? Planning is a hard thing to do but not impossible, if you know what the future should look like then you can better manage your own life.

But being a good planner is not that difficult, you can find help all over the web, in books and even asking professionals can be a very good way to learn how to plan your schedule. For Example, Janet White in her article "How to be a good planner in 10 easy steps" gives us a guide to be more organized. (1)

The first step consists on getting a life. An important part of our life is what we do outside work. Since work can be extremely time consuming you need to focus on organizing your life first and then try to organize your business life. Having time for your family, friends and for yourself is necessary since an excess of work can lead to health issues and a separation from society. Taking work home, staying after hours and simply worrying too much about work is very dangerous for a business person since it can absorb you and will not let you pay attention to the more important aspects of your life. I agree completely, sometimes it is a matter of having other people tell you you're a workaholic when you simply can't notice it.

If you want to have an organized business life, if you want your business to follow a plan you set up then you have to start by applying all this to your life. If you are unemployed set yourself the goal of getting a job. How to do it?

Look for ads, go to interviews, get a degree, and call a few friends. Simply list the steps necessary for the goal to be accomplished. Plan your days accordingly, spend time with your family and loved ones after work.

Once you have organized your life you can start organizing yourself in the business world and plan. What happens if you have a meeting and a soccer match at the same time on the same day? What happens if your car breaks down on your way to work? A person is the same in the workplace as he is in the household. Be mindful of that and keep your plans straight.

Second and in my opinion one of the most important steps is to control stress. When controlling stress everyone has a different approach. Some people like to play videogames, others like to exercise, and some like to have a nice meal, laugh with friends, or whatever floats your boat. But I believe managing stress means avoiding it. For example, if you know you have a paper due Friday at 5 P.M. why wait until Thursday night to do it? Why if you have a report due for Monday you don't start building it by pieces whenever you are idle. Managing stress sometimes means managing your time as well. We can also say that managing stress means having everything organized and knowing that you are on the right track and that you can get everything done. Don't be scared of deadlines, simply manage your time effectively and try to remain calm, even if you feel you are stressed. Try to tell people you are stressed; they can have good tips for it and sometimes help you deal with it.

On the topic on letting other people know you are stressed comes networking. In the world of business you will get to know lots of people with similar interests to yours. Some will not share your ideas but you can't have everyone like you.

If you start to create connections and networks you can then have other people help you. You can have other companies take some of the load off through outsourcing. Have a friend create the supply chain that your company needs to get all your products on time. If two heads think better than one then imagine what a bunch of heads with the same ideal can accomplish . . . once they can agree on something that is. Knowing people, having mentors lead you in the right track is also pretty useful as you have a sense of direction when you start in a company.

It is also helpful to join some type or organization that can help you create connections, tat way if you get fired you can fall back into the people you have made friendship with so they can offer you a position or come up with a business idea. I don't really believe in business organizations or places like the "20-30's" or the "Leones" here in Panama. Since we are talking about Panama what they all want is to talk about women and have a beer.

Still you need to keep yourself up to date with new technologies in business. In the ever changing industry there can exist many technologies that can help you make work easier. Easier work means less stress, it also means you can complete it faster so you can dedicate time to other priorities. Staying educated can be challenging but as new executives are born into the technology age it is easier for them to understand and adapt to new technologies.

The best way to be up to date with new technologies and market trends is to read. Even if you don't have time, the web is filled with different magazines that can keep you informed. You can even find out about other people's way of planning you can imitate them, when you see the market trends you can plan what your company will do and when you have all things figured out you can move ahead better.

Being a good planner means having the energy to accomplish the goals you have set yourself. Your need to get inspired in every task you make, inspiration can make the difference between a good and an excellent work. By inspiration I mean that you have to put all your effort in the task at hand. It's a feeling you have that makes you move forward and finish the work. If you do the task without giving it your all then you might find yourself in the situation that you don't want to keep on moving.

Sometimes stress is a great factor that will keep you from doing the tasks you need. Stress can cut your inspiration when you remember the many things you still have to do. People sometimes "close down" to the rest of the world and end up doing nothing. Inspiration sometimes also means doing work while listening to some music, having certain images in front of you to help you stay motivated is always helpful but people will need to check their company's policies regarding such types of entertainment since they sometime are more of a distraction.

If you know all the details of the work you need to do then it is easier to be organized and therefore be better planned. Knowing who to contact, why should you contact him and when keeps you on track and once you make the plan everything will start falling into place. It's very different to think "I have to give this report to someone on accounting" than "I have to give this to Larry from accounting because he manages budgets". You can then make a budget heavy report and specifically tell Larry what you need to achieve your plan for the company. It also helps to have people think you are indispensable since they will then go to you and you can know the dealings of the company, making planning so much easier.

This is where strategic relationships come into play. You may go to parties and start to make business contacts with people who you know will be helpful in the future. Knowing who owns what and who can get you that special item you need is very significant. Making acquaintance with powerful business people has opened the path to many employees that started in low positions and gradually moved up. When you want a good plan made always give the right work to the right person so they are capable of performing exactly what you need.

We also emphasize on teamwork. Since knowing who to give the work to is crucial you also need to work together with the people in your company. But not only that, if your company relies on a supplier then a strong supply chain is important too. Things you don't know can be easily accomplished by others; they can detect mistakes you don't easily see and even help you plan. Pointing at mistakes as well as giving alternatives from other points of view is one of the main reasons why being a team player is an important step to become a good planner. No person can work alone in a company and sometimes you have to rely on other in certain moments.

Getting everything written down is also a good way to organize. That way you don't miss steps, you can know where you are going and everything can make more sense of organization. Writing down your plan and the steps you are going to take in order to make it will help you see the whole plan so you can pin point the bottlenecks, the errors and the different possibilities that can branch from your objectives. Planning technologies can help a lot too in easing up the time it takes to plan and better organize it.

Planning is a vital part of business, being a better planner is something all those of us who want to go into the world of business should learn how to do. Having an idea of what you have to accomplish and where you want to go.

Your business will surely benefit from a good business plan and your life will be greatly enhanced by planning ahead what you want to accomplish. Organizing, networking, being indispensable and knowing your direction some of the aspects you need to develop in order to help you become a better planner.

Technology is important, knowing your market is also important and Forecasting can be very helpful when you are trying to plan for the future. You should always be mindful of those around you and always try to think more in the future than in the present. If the situation allows it, always try to move one step at a time, manage stress properly and keep yourself inspired as much as you can. Life is short, there is no time for new plans.

In business knowing where you are going means being one step ahead than the others. Communicating your ideas as a manager, leader or entrepreneur will surely help you when you want to make these ideas happen. Showing people you are sure of where you are going as well as being able to manage stress effectively will surely make you a better entrepreneur and open many doors wherever you walk.

VI-D
Planning as an important management tool

Planning is a great tool for anyone who wants to succeed in life. I believe that having an idea of what you are going to do is a good start to get things done right. Of course this does not mean that we have to know exactly every detail and step of the process but at least a brief idea to begin. Eventually, the plans you have made might change but it will be easier to have a guide at first than nothing at all. This tool will also help you to break a big complex goal into small manageable tasks that together will get you to the big final goal. By planning you are making things easier for yourself.

For business it is exactly the same thing as for your personal life, I think in both areas planning become a very important part of them and creates the base in which you will work. Before I though that planning was not for me, I am a very disorganize person and I just get things done as it goes; all that mindset has changed now because I realize that I could do things better if I plan them. At the beginning I did not how to start but what I realize was that I could actually organize task in general without being that specific which is the most difficult part for me. Having everything planned perfectly is not really my style but what I did noticed is that planning is not about know everything you are going to do. Planning is more like general ideas that will help you complete your goal.

According to Stephen P. Robbins an Timothy A. Judge on their four edition of their book called organizational behavior; "In the early part of the twentieth, French industrialist Henri Fayol wrote that all managers perform five management functions: planning, organizing, commanding, coordinating and controlling. Today we have condensed these to four: planning, organizing, leading and controlling"[3] As you can notice planning has always been an important tool for manager, it is the first point they have to develop when they are doing any project. It has been that way for many years and many research had support this idea. As a company you want to have the best managers who can handle and improve the performance of the business that is why the workplace it is always full of goal and points to reach, as a good manager or even better, as a good leader you will have to develop the skill of planning because it will guide you through the entire road.

"Planning is a process that includes defining goals, establishing strategy, and developing plans to coordinate activities"[4] As the definition says goals are always needed for developing this tool. It is very important that a person as a manager or a leader know where they are going to, what they are heading. The first step in all this process will be to have the goal well defined; it is the most important things. As simple as you cannot do something you don't know you are doing. It works in the same way as personal life because you have a set of desire and things you want to get, planning gets a role when you have to develop steps to follow and complete what you are expecting.

Imagine anything you want to accomplish, set a goal and think on what you are going to do to accomplish it. What you are doing at that moment is planning how things are going to get done. At a personal level you might do it mentally and you wont write anything down but at a company level the series of steps you are going to use needs to be written and most of the time send it to your supervisor/boss. Probably that is one of the main reasons why the company hired you, they want you to make things easier for them; and planning is a perfect way of separating the big picture to get easier tasks to complete.

Planning can be a very stressful subject because it will required patient and time but at the end it will be very worth it because it will makes things easier for your boss, subordinates and even yourself. "Noted author Mark Twain hit it on the head when he said: The Secret of getting ahead is getting started. The secret of getting started

---

[3]   Judge, Timothy A. "1." *Organizational Behavior*. By Stephen P. Robbins. Fourteenth ed. 5-7. Print.
[4]   Ibídem

is breaking your complex overwhelming tasks into small manageable ones—then starting on the first one."[5] The best way of doing things is by starting by the easiest part, and as the quote says this is practically what planning it is all about. Make it simple, separate task, breaking the whole picture. This quote perfectly describes the goal of planning and how useful it will be for you to become a planner.

The question now is why planning is such an important tool in both areas life and business. We can begin with a really good point, which is productivity. Every company in the world is looking for productivity so employees must find a way to generate profit to the company otherwise, you they will be fired because they are not meeting expectations. Planning and productivity are very related because if you organize the goals into several easier tasks it will be easier and faster to complete them and this will generate productivity for the company. That is why very important to understand the meaning of planning and how to implement it. More planning equals more productivity.

Another important point of this important tool is that it will facilitate the decision making process in any business. Once you have all the steps planned it will be easier for you or your boss to analyze the project and come up with decision if it is necessary. The decision making process is a very important part of a project because if the decision is the correct one then the project will succeed. Having a good plan will help you to decide on the best option possible, which will end on a successful project accomplishment.

On the other hand, the possibility of failure on the project will decline if a good plan has been made. The future is more predictable and the percentage of having a crisis will be very low. Even though having a plan seems like you already know what is going to happen, it is important to have a plan B just in case something happen. It is a way of protecting the company for any risk possible.

Planning will also help you to focus on personal energy direction. When I say your personal energy I mean that by making a plan you can better focus on the tasks to reach the final outcome. You energy will make accomplish the goal in a more timely and efficient manner.

---

5   "Why Is Planning Important?" *Submit Articles or Find Free Articles*. Web. 29 Apr. 2011. <http://www.articlealley.com/article_32151_36.html>.

It is important to also mention that this important management tool will also eliminate bad habits and the fear of failure. If you follow a plan you are more likely to loose some bad habits like fooling around without accomplish your tasks. This is a very common problem in the workplace today that is why planning had become so important and useful for managers. Sticking to a plan will also help you not to miss any task and you will be less likely to fail. That is very important because it is one of the main things companies are looking for; they need employees who commit the fewer amounts of mistakes when accomplishing their goals.

There is also an important part of planning that will be very useful for everyone in the workplace and in his or her personal life. Procrastination has always been an issue for many employees, it is common to see them overwhelmed and confused about what tasks must be done first. Establishing priorities is very important when it comes to efficiency; you need to know what you come first, what is urgent and what it is not. The easiest way of reaching that point is by implementing the planning tool, which will separate the outcome in small manageable tasks and you will be able to choose the most important or urgent and start from there. In that way the goal will be accomplish efficiently.

On the workplace as in personal life they are always some issues and things that happen that we cannot control and were not planned. Developing any project anything can went wrong and it is important to have a second plan and know what to do on those situations. Remember that being ahead of the problem will help you to solve it faster. It is important to have another plan that will back up the one you are implementing just in case something goes wrong.

"Planning permits managers to examine and analyze alternative course of action with a better understanding of their likely consequences. If managers have an enhanced awareness of the possible future effects of alternative courses of action, for making a decision or for taking any action, they will be able to exercise judgment and proceed cautiously to choose the most feasible and favorable course of action"[6] As a manager

---

[6]   "Importance of Planning." *HubPages*. Web. 29 Apr. 2011. <http://hubpages.com/hub/Importance-of-Planning>.

it is your job to decide the best path to develop the project and the best way to do it is by planning. Separate the big outcome into small tasks, pick the most important first and start from there. This will also help if one subordinate need help at some point it will be easier for the manager to help them by looking at the plan and see what is the critical point and come up with ideas to solve it.

I believe planning is a very important tool in the management field because it is one of the first steps you must follow for becoming an efficient manager. You cannot start from the end, always from the beginning. Sometimes many managers fail in creating a good plan and if they plan wrong then all the next steps will also be wrong. It is like the construction of a building if the bases of the construction are not strong enough then the whole building will fall down. In business planning is like creating that cushion in which your project will lay on. As a manager you will have to manage people and they will depend on you and your decisions, it is important to be clear about what you are doing so your subordinates can understand their tasks and accomplish them in the right way. As their boss you are seeing as a reliable person in whom they can rely on.

As time passes new ideas and technologies are coming up. In the business world it works in the same way. For example the perception of planning has changed within the years. Before it was not that important but now it is; that is why many software companies are creating planning software for business. It is becoming more easier for managers to plan nowadays than it used to be some years ago, and not only for a manager but for any employee. Obviously managers must be the first ones planning but also subordinates must plan in smaller scales. Once managers and subordinates both are correctly planning then the work will be more efficient. As planning is becoming more important and useful, many companies are developing planning software's that will help businesses to efficiently plan. This is a great tool for managers because it will make the planning part easier which is the key part for a successful project.

One of the main problems in businesses right now it is the way in which decisions are made. Many time decisions need to be made in very short time period with lack of information, for a manager this a challenging tasks but he or she must confront them almost every day. In order to choose the best option it is important for them to at least have the outcome separate in different tasks again they need to plan. Of course even by planning mistakes can be made but the idea is to reduce the room for error.

I believe one of the main advantages of planning will be the group integration, in the workplace team work is a every day meal; you are always working and relating to other people in the company; managers and subordinates, people on top of you and people below. Teamwork is the key point of success as much integrate is the group the better and more efficient the accomplish will be. Here is when planning takes place once again. "**Integration:** Planning is an important process to bring about effective integration of the diverse decisions and activities of the managers not only at a point of time but also over a period of time"[7] Integration between different decision and activities will also end up in group integration, which will help in the performance of the tasks they are working on.

After analyzed and looked close to the importance of planning we can see into how the planning process works. This process consist on 8 steps that you must follow in order to develop a plan, those steps will lead you to the accomplishment of the final goal you working on. You can see the planning process on the Annexes in figure 1.

Stage 1: Analysis of opportunities: "One approach to this is to examine your current position, and decide how you can improve it. There are a number of techniques that will help you to do this: SWOT Analysis, Risk analysis and understanding pressure for change"[8] The idea on this phase is to realize first where you are standing, remember that in order to find the problem you need to analyze yourself first. In this case analyze the company or the project depending on the goal you are reaching.

---

[7]   Ibídem

[8]   "The Planning Cycle - Project Management Tools from MindTools. com." *Mind Tools - Management Training, Leadership Training and Career Training*. Web. 29 Apr. 2011. <http://www.mindtools.com/pages/article/ newPPM_05.htm

Stage 2:   Identifying the Aim of your plan: "decide precisely what the aim of your plan is. Deciding and defining an aim sharpens the focus of your plan, and helps you to avoid wasting effort on irrelevant side issues."[9] It is very important to know where you are going; you need to have a specific goal. When you are planning it is very important to have a very clear idea of the tasks you are heading. This can be called as a vision or mission statement.

Stage 3:   Exploring options: Once you already know where you are going the next step is to create different options of how to do it. On this stage you will need a lot of creativity to come up with different ideas regarding the goal. The idea is to generate as many options as possible, the more option you have the easier is to really choose the best one.

Stage 4:   Selecting the best option: Once you have all the alternatives you need to choose the best one for accomplish your goal. If you have the resources and time you might first evaluate each of them and finally decide upon one of them. It will be more accurate if you first evaluate them and then select one, but this opportunity will not always be available; sometimes you must decide without previous evaluation.

Stage 5:   Detailed Planning: "Detailed planning is the process of working out the most efficient and effective way of achieving the aim that you have defined"[10] On this stage you already choose an option and now you have to decide what, when, where, how and why you are going to develop the option you have chosen.

Stage 6.   Evaluation of the Plan and its Impact: Once you have developed the plan then you need to evaluate if it going to work and how it will affect the employees, the company and the project. This stage is very important because according to the result you will get from this you will decide on implementing the plan or not.

---

[9]   Ibídem
[10]   **Ibídem**

Stage 7:   Implementing change: Now you have proved the plan and look into the consequences of doing it. In stage number 7 it is time for taking action and implementing the plan with all the steps you have done before. The plan should tell you exactly what you must do and you will even have to monitor the execution of the plan later on.

Stage 8:   Closing the plan: Once you are done with the plan you can close the project. It is always good to evaluate how did all the process went and see if you can change or improve during any stage of it.

This planning process can be called more as a cycle because you might go back and change some parts while you are doing it. You can always go back and model the cycle in the best way that suits you. After discussing the importance of planning and the planning cycle we can now have an idea on how useful is to plan when you want to reach any goal. This is not only for projects on businesses but also in your personal life. "If you fail to plan, to plan to fail."

CHAPTER VII

Organization

When you begin a business, you begin a challenge that is unlike any other. Suddenly your life is much more complicated than you ever thought it would be. The case is certainly no different with a food concession business. Some may think that it is much easier to deal with, but that is just not the case. While the concession trailer business is a difficult undertaking no matter what you do, there are many things that you can do to make your life easier. One of the most important traits to make sure that you perfect when opening and running any business is organization. Developing your organizational skills can help you have a much easier time with paperwork, routine for business, and can make your life easier in general.

The first thing that getting organized can do for you is to give you help with your paperwork. Keeping track of income, expenditures and taxes is all a part of running a successful business. Coming up with an organizational system can help obliterate confusion. Having receipts, ticket books, and an up-to-date list of income and expenditures cuts down on clutter as well. Plus, when you need to find something, you can go right to the items you are looking for because they are well organized. There are several systems out there that you can put into place for your concession business. There are electronic tracking systems available or you can come up with a system that is all your own that can work for you. Taxes are something you must keep very close track of or it becomes difficult to prepare them when the time comes.

Payroll is something else that organization can aid with if you have employees.

Organization doesn't just come in handy with regard to paperwork. It can also help when you are dealing with inventory and daily and weekly business routines. Listing the things you expect from your business operations and from your employees is a great way to make sure everything gets done when it is supposed to. Also, having a system for the stocking and restocking of inventory can make the business run a lot more smoothly. If you don't have a system in place, do some research. The internet is a fantastic source of information. Also, asking people in this line of work the way that they handle their businesses can be of tremendous help.

Organization is not simply for the business world. It can make your overall life better in general. Organizing your life will make things easier to find, save you time, and could even save you money. Wasting time looking for things you've misplaced and forgetting to take that defective product back to the store can cost you two of the most valuable commodities that exist. Time and money don't grow on trees and if you take the time to organize and then you keep it that way, they are two commodities you don't have to worry about losing. Organizing your business can bring you the same benefit, in a much bigger way. The value of your time is more and the money you stand to lose is a much higher amount. The price for being disorganized in your business is definitely a hefty one.

VII-A
Organizational Behavior Importance

Organizations are all around us. We are born in an organization, we live, work and most probably will die in an organization. Yet most of us do not understand how people function, behave and interact between each other within these organizations. We also do not understand if people shape an organization or an organization shapes people.

In the beginning, people create an organization and shape its mission and culture and later more people join the organization. This new group of people adjust themselves within the existing organizational culture.

Sometimes they also influence organizational culture by bringing new and unique skills to the organization. Sometimes they learn from each and at other times, external forces like competition, political and cultural changes compel them to learn new technical, communication or interpersonal skills. All these internal and external factors help an organization and its people to evolve to cope with the ever-changing world.

Until recently, managers paid little attention to Organizational Behavior or soft skill training. The industrial revolution created the need for hard (technical) skills. People worked in the production line and were not required to think or interact to each other. However, things have changed; instead of standing behind the production lines, they now sit in front of a computer and control a robot who works in the production line. Now, people need more technical skills, but they also need skills to communicate and work within a group.

The great English poet Samuel Butler put it together more eloquently, "Any fool can paint a picture, but it takes a wise man to be able to sell it." If the "fool" is the metaphor for hard skill then the "wise man" would be the soft skill; but the soft skill of the wise man is useless without the hard skill of the fool; the harmonizing of both skills sells the picture. Therefore, the study of Organizational Behavior is not considered pop psychobabble anymore. A comparison between old and new organizations makes the picture clear.

Old Organization vs. New Organization

In his book *Power Up: Transforming Organizations Through Shared Responsibility Leadership,* Stanford professor of Organizational Behavior David L. Bradford pointed out three major distinctions between an old static organization and new organization powered by Interpersonal Dynamics (cited in Zich, 1998).

First, in old organizations, machinery used to be considered as a primary asset, and in order to maximize productivity the managers needed to concentrate on 100% usage of those machinery. Later, people became the most important asset of the new organization and organizations are finding ways to use the "whole person". According to Bradford, within last ten years, usage of human capital raised from 20 percent to 40 percent. Second, in the new organization everyone is responsible for the whole process. The old organizational attitude was "you are responsible for your area and I'm responsible for mine and if you screwed up, that helps me to look better." But the new organizational attitude is all about "powering up", according to Bradford, "increasing the total power of each individual, every unit, and the entire organization." Old organizational layers are slowly melting together and the words 'superior' and 'subordinate' are becoming obsolete. For example, in my company, everyone has the same title 'benefits consultant' and the difference between managers and consultants is defined by the word 'senior'. Finally, in the old organization it was always presumed that the bosses know the solution to all problems; according to Bradford, "the traditional organization is anti-learning." In the old organization, managers used to show up in the meetings with a solution. New organizations are constantly evolving and in this new environment, managers are not ashamed to admit they need input and assistance.

The new organizational paradigm—people focused thinking which is based on healthy communications and supportive leadership (Hayes, 2001), has been receiving a lot of attention in recent years. At the same time, the demand for hard skills has also increased—the technologically advanced society demands more analytically and technologically savvy workforce. Therefore, the challenge is to develop human capital with the perfect combinations of hard and soft skills. Political economist Robert Reich recommended the hi-tech companies to focus more on human capital than high volume production. He said in order to attract employees and reduce turnover, companies must create an environment that fosters learning and responsibility and encourage group ownership in a common mission (cited in Ricadela, 2000).

Therefore, the previously perceived notion that this hi-tech, high paced environment would cause stiff cutthroat competition among workers and create tyrannical corporate environment never materialized. Instead, we are observing more and more cooperation and support among workers.

OB Importance—Some Evidence

Recent research shows that soft skill training should start at the University. Graham and Krueger (1996) pointed out that soft skills are not well-appreciated and understood among students—students consider decision making, computer and math competencies as the most important skills. However, in an extensive study done on career paths of corporate CFOs by Baker and Phillips (1999) shows high level of importance put on soft skills by the CFOs. The following table (Baker & Phillips, 1999, p. 48) shows the most important skills that someone should acquire to be a CFO:

Skill	Percentage
Communication (Oral and Written)	13.3%
Management and Leadership	12.4
Financial (e.g. Cash Management and Financial Analysis)	10.1
People and Interpersonal	9.5
Analytical and Critical Thinking	9.1
Technical (e.g., Mathematics and Statistics)	7.4
Accounting and Taxation	6.3
Computer	4.4
Negotiation	1.7
Other (e.g., Foreign Language, Strategic Planning and Organizational Skills)	25.7
Total	100.0%

The next table (Baker & Phillips, 1999, p. 48) shows the gaps between what business schools teach and what companies need for entry-level finance positions:

Gap	Percentage
Real World and Work Experience	17.2%
Communication Skills (Oral and Written)	13.3
Management and Leadership Skills	6.7
People and Interpersonal Skills	7.7
Financial Skills (e.g., Cash Management)	4.9
Accounting and Taxation Skills	5.9

Analytical and Critical Thinking Skills	4.2
Computer Skills (e.g., Spreadsheet)	3.9
Ethics	2.8
Other (e.g., Self-Development, Investment Theory)	33.3
Total	100.0%

Conclusion

To summarize the researches on OB, there is more evidence that the teaching and implementation of soft skills should get higher priority in education and company training process, but it should only complement hard skill, not substitute for it.

Today's postindustrial hi-tech organization requires knowledge intensive work environment and demands creativity form its workers. Most organizations are now encouraging team approach to solve problems. Workers are not only need to learn new technical skills but also how to communicate, delegate, negotiate, and motivate with each other.

CHAPTER VIII

Prioritization

"Balance and peace of mind follow the person who develops a clear sense of his or her highest priorities and who lives focus and integrity toward them" (Stephen R. Covey).

Today, life is more complex, more stressful, more demanding and absolutely exhausting. We have transitioned from the industrial age to the information worker age, with all of its profound consequences. We face challenges and problems in our personal and professional lives. (1).

Many people take on more responsibility than they should and there never seems to be enough hours in the day to complete the tasks and projects collecting dust on the top of your desk. How do you decide which task is really the most important at any given time? Is it the one that's most urgent, the one that will earn you the most money, the one that will produce the greatest long-term happiness or the one that will please your boss the most? We all ask those questions ourselves every single day; the answer is that you must learn how to focus your energy on your top priority tasks.

Prioritization refers to that process of classifying our goals and tasks, in order to be productive and get things done; however, most of the people face a big challenge called—Procrastination that refers to the human act of postponing or delaying a task. It presents many causes and rationalizations, from distractions, lack of motivation, perfectionism and laziness to fear of success or failure (2).

In our busy world we have so many things to do that we reach a point when we can't say any more which tasks are more important than others. The result of not prioritizing our goals and acts make us to postpone many important things. This happens because all we have to do come in our mind at the same time. If we don't classify them in order of importance, all we can do is just to pick one; usually we pick the easiest and pleasant, not the important one.

Learning how to prioritize your activities helps you focus on important activities first, which are your high-value activities; prioritization allows you to complete the most important tasks before engaging in low-value activities. According to the Italian economists, Vilfredo Pareto, this is relevant to the 80/20 rule where mentioned that around 80% of outputs are a result of 20% of input (3). So, if you can draw all your energy and learn techniques on how to focus on the 20% of your tasks early in the day, you'll get 80% of return by investing your time to complete the 20% of activities. For example, if you have 100 tasks in your task list, probably about 20 of those will be the key ones to focus on.

Learning how to prioritize is one of the most important time management tools you can use to increase your personal efficiency and is the essential skill you need to make the very best use of your own efforts. Furthermore, it is particularly important when time is limited and demands are seemingly unlimited. With good prioritization you can bring order to chaos, massively reduce stress, and move towards a successful conclusion.

When you find yourself with too many things to do and not enough time to do them, stress rises. So, instead of trying to schedule it all in, you should take some time to identify your priorities. Then, you should focus your energies on what matters the most to you. By modifying the amount and type of things you do, you experience more pleasure in your work, less stress, and more personal satisfaction. Prioritizing effectively is obligatory to growth for organizations and for individual development. When you prioritize, you eliminate the stress that comes from being disorganized and overwhelmed, and you move forward in the direction you want to go in your life.

Although it sounds simple, there is more involved with prioritization than deciding what to do next. Successful prioritization requires the execution of a carefully designed plan. For prioritization to have any meaning, it's imperative that you have a clear objective. Your personal objective may be a set of goals, your mission statement or purpose, or even a state of being. The role of prioritization then is to help you achieve this result with as little effort as possible.

To become more prioritized the first step you need to take is to **plan your day ahead of time.** It's impossible to prioritize when you have no clear idea of what needs to be done. Second, you must make a List of the things and tasks you need to accomplish, and write down all of the things that are on your mind. The important thing is to get all of them on paper and to consolidate all of your little lists into a single, comprehensive to-do list; on this list you'll place the big activities and chores but also the smaller tasks and obligations. After completing the list you need to eliminate any things that are based only on wants. If the item is not something that is absolutely necessary but you'd really like to do it, place it at the bottom of the list; transfer all of the other non-essential items to another list (you can do them once you've completed the items on your main list). To keep to-do lists under control, you need to rate each task in order of importance Moreover, do not accept responsibility for completing other people's work. If you are busy doing work that other people should be doing, you won't have enough time to complete your own responsibilities. Also, don't be ashamed to ask for help to complete your assignments, it is all right to ask for assistance; that's how you cultivate relationships and build teamwork within a company. However, in life and business environment priorities change every day. As a result, you need to constantly reassess your to-do list to keep up with your changing priorities.

The third and very important step is identifying deadlines for each task. You must estimate the time it will take for you to accomplish each task. You should allow a few extra minutes for each task, just in case they take longer than you expect. Also, it is critical to consider whether there is something on the list that must be completed before something else, because knowing what is most important to you allows you to devote your energy on your priorities. Beside each item on the list, you should write down its actual due date; you shouldn't establish due dates based on when you would like to have them completed but, on when the task is actually required to be completed. Any item that would create negative consequences if not completed should be given very high priority.

At your work environment, a great technique that will make you look and feel better is giving yourself extra time when asked for a deadline. If you think something will take three days, tell them you need five. Then, deliver it in three and they will think you are very conscientious.

The power of focus is the key to success; you must focus your energies on the task at hand and do nothing else. To do that you must eliminate any interruptions or distractions that might interfere with your flow; for example co-workers, phone calls, e-mails, Internet and so on. Furthermore, Keep your list in a prominent area so you'll see it frequently, and do your best to stick to the plan you've set for yourself.

Time management is the process of exercising conscious control over the amount of time spent on specific activities, especially to increase efficiency. Time management may be aided by a range of skills, tools, and techniques used to <u>manage</u> time when accomplishing specific tasks, projects and goals.

When you have to choose among several tasks, there are several helpful prioritization methods you can use. First, Stephen R. Covey, in his book *The Seven Habits of Highly Effective People,* describes a high-level prioritization scheme. In this scheme, tasks are categorized by four quadrants: QI—Important and Urgent, QII—Important but Not Urgent, QIII—Not Important but Urgent, QIV—Not Important and Not Urgent. Dr. Covey notes that highly effective people make time for the QII activities, and that doing so can reduce the time spent in other quadrants. (4)

Second, the ABC Method. An early advocate of "ABC" prioritization was Alan Lakein. In his system "A" items were the most important, "B" next most important, "C" least important. Then it subdivides tasks in these categories into A1, A2, A3, B1, B2 and so forth. A lot of people find this prioritization method to be very helpful. (5)

Third, the Payoff versus Time Method. With this method, you weight each task by the payoff you expect from it versus the time it takes to do it. Tasks that have high payoff and that take little time are the ones you would do first. Correspondingly, tasks that have low payoff and that take a lot of time are ones you would do last or not at all (6).

Forth, the Paired Comparison method. This method uses a simple scoring system for comparing activities. Paired Comparison Analysis helps you to set priorities where there are conflicting demands on your resources. It is also an ideal tool for comparing completely different options such as whether to invest in marketing, a new IT system or a new piece of machinery. (7)

Fifth, the POSEC method. POSEC stands for the initial letters of Prioritize by Organizing, Streamlining, Economizing and Contributing. The method dictates a template which emphasizes an average individual's immediate sense of emotional and monetary security. It suggests that by attending to one's personal responsibilities first, an individual is better positioned to shoulder collective responsibilities. According to POSEC, you need to Prioritize Your time and define your life by goals, then you need to Organize the Things you have to accomplish regularly, to be successful; Streamlining things you may not like to do, but must do; Economizing Things you should do or may even like to do, but they're not pressingly urgent; and Contributing, By paying attention to the few remaining things that make a difference (8).

Nowadays, **it's easy for smart, creative people to generate lots of good ideas for projects.** The problem is that if you're not careful, you can easily have more projects going than you have people, time, and money to complete them. When your list of pending projects becomes overwhelming, you've got to figure out how to sort through them and prioritize them.

A Generic Approach to Prioritizing Projects is a 3-step approach. First, you **determine your criteria and create a ranking scale** for discriminating among projects; for example, **Strategic Value, Ease, Financial Benefit, Cost and Resource Impact. Second, you make a grid or table with the names of your prioritization criteria across the top and the names of potential projects down the left column. And third, you review each project and apply a value for each of the criteria. Then add you up the total scores for each project and determine their priority (9).**

For example, a Prioritization Matrix is a useful technique you can use with your team members to achieve consensus about an issue. The Matrix helps you rank problems or issues, usually generated through brainstorming, by a particular criterion that is important to your organization. Then you can more clearly see which problems are the most important to work on solving first. Prioritization matrix helps to consider the opinion of everyone in a brainstorming session, as well as to give weight to various criteria and prioritize pressing problems over others. This helps determine which problems need to be solved first in order to meet organizational objectives.

Several steps must be taken in creating a prioritization matrix. First, Brainstorming, where you identify the problems which need to be addressed and identify the key criteria on the basis of which these problems are to be evaluated. Second, you **draw the Prioritization Matrix Chart (10).** In the first column, you list down the problems which have been identified in the brainstorming session; and from the 2nd column onwards you list down the criteria for evaluation along with their weight age. Third, is ranking the problems; you make all the participants rank each of the problems on a pre-determined scale against each of the evaluation criteria. Last step is to calculate the **total results. You** compute the total ranking for each problem and this helps obtain a prioritized list of problems to work upon (11).

Another example is the 9-square tool that is being used in determining how to prioritize different projects. The 9-square is a prioritization tool in Lean problem solving that helps you organize your improvement ideas. The 9-square gives a visual representation of where projects fall relative to each other. First you conduct a brainstorming session in which you compile a large number of viable options; then, you have to decide which ones to implement. To use the 9-square, you rank each in two categories: impact and ease of implementation. Afterwards, you create a 3 x 3 grid, with low, medium, and high impact as the vertical scale. Hard, medium, and easy to implement go on the horizontal scale. After doing so, you place your options into the appropriate boxes. You might have to choose between two similarly valued proposals; for example, would you rather do a medium impact, but easy project, or a high impact project that will require medium effort? You run into a few of these situations, but generally, you will end up with the most desirable project being at the top right, and the worst options at the lower left (12).

In conclusion, many people think that if they are busy it means they are productive. Unfortunately, being busy does not mean you are productive. You can be busy doing the wrong things and never get closer to your goals.

Clarifying what you value most will help you prioritize efficiently your tasks. We need to ensure our priorities are consistent with our personal goals and the goals of our organizations. Learning how to prioritize is one of the most important time management tools you can use to increase your personal efficiency.

Setting priorities is critical to success. When you prioritize, you ask the questions about the importance of the tasks. Taking the time to consider your priorities takes only a few minutes; it makes a world of difference. It allows you to organize your thoughts and to manage your life and your work with intention and purpose. This means you get more done in less time and you feel good because you're in control. When you feel as though you're in control, you experience more <u>peace</u> and you're able to focus with greater intensity.

You are in charge of your time. You have to use it wisely. Prioritizing is an art and you become better at that with practice. The power is yours to choose using the right tools and succeed in your life. The real challenge is not manage time, but manage ourselves.

VIII—A
The Importance of Knowing How to Prioritize

One of the key elements that every person must have in their hands in order to succeed and progress in life is knowing how to manage their time. In order to be successful in the way you manage your time and activities you must first know a thing or two about prioritization. So, what is prioritization? First of all, there are two ways in which one can define prioritization. The first one, is viewing it as a principle in which case prioritizing will be to do "first things first". The second option is to view prioritization as a process in which case, it means evaluating a group of items and ranking them in their order of importance or urgency. Either way, it comes down to the same thing, we all have tasks or duties that are more important than others and yet many times we fail, and fall into the temptation of the other secondary things that tend to be more appealing and/or fun. It is of my interest that in the upcoming pages you achieve a deep and precise understanding of:

➢ What is prioritization?
➢ Why is it important?
➢ How to become successful at prioritizing?

I cannot emphasize enough on how important it is for us as human beings to set priorities and to know how to remain loyal to them. It is because of people having the wrong priorities that many times wrong and unexpected things happen. Having the wrong priorities tends to go hand in hand with making the wrong decisions or going for the wrong choices. It is because of lack of priorities that some people may come to find themselves lost, dazed, and confused in their lives. This is why I am writing this right now, in order for people to be able to see how important it is to know that if it comes down to studying for an exam or going to a party, studying for this exam will have much more benefits than going to one single party for one night. The previous example is just one of the many in which someone's priorities can go wrong. There are many priorities in life and each one of these priorities holds a different value for each one of us; a list of some of these priorities follows:

➢ Marriage
➢ Career
➢ Children
➢ Health/Fitness
➢ Religion/Spirituality
➢ Travel
➢ Sports
➢ Friends/Social Engagements
➢ Hobbies
➢ Community Service

One of the main problems is that we try to achieve excellence in all areas of our lives, we want to be successful at work and we want to give our families the time and dedication that they deserve. After a time it becomes obvious that perfection in every aspect of our lives is impossible. It is when we realize this that we become angry and frustrated, so this is why according to Henrik Edberg in his book *The Art of Relaxed Productivity,* "we should try prioritizing as a tool to bring you to happiness and fulfillment." Life today presents so many distractions, and therefore, it is very easy to lose time on unimportant activities. Ask yourself, is watching this or that TV program, reading this or that gossip or participating in a certain activity is going to add anything to your life. Is the time spent on an activity well spent, or is just a waste of time and energy? It is here where having well set up priorities becomes important. A person with the wrong priorities or no priorities what so ever, will probably choose going to a party rather than studying for an exam. We must train ourselves to be able to distinguish between things that will mean something in the end and things that will add no value to our lives. This person who chose to go to a party instead of studying for his or her exam will probably wake up the following morning not knowing what on earth to do. This is why another important reason why we should prioritize is that setting priorities has proven to dramatically reduce our stress. Making the wrong decisions can literally make us or break us and if we don't know how to prioritize we will not know what is right and what is wrong which, is crucial in our lives in order to become well-formed, successful individuals.

Speaking from my own experience, me being a twenty-one year old woman I can tell you I have had my struggles with setting priorities many, many times indeed. What I found to be one of the main things that kept me from sticking to the priorities I had set was this annoying thing call "procrastination". Procrastination, according to the Merriam Webster's online dictionary, refers to the act of replacing high-priority actions with tasks of low-priority, and thus putting off important tasks to a later time. This brings me back to what I said before; you need to know your priorities so that you can then be able to organize them in order of importance. What matters is what these priorities mean to you and this is why you do not necessarily have to have the same priorities as your friends or family because everything has a different meaning for everybody. I have learned that setting priorities frees me from unwise decisions, from saying "yes" when I need to say "no," and keeps me on the course toward my goals. Everyone procrastinates. We put things off because we don't want to do them, or because we have too many other things that we could be doing. Putting things off big or small is part of being human. However, you must understand that there are things in life that you are required to accomplish and that you cannot avoid them simply because you do not want to them. In order to overcome procrastination, in his book The Now Habit, Dr. Neil Fiore suggests that making time for guaranteed fun could be an effective way to overcome procrastination. Decide in advance what blocks of time you'll have each week for family time, entertainment, exercise, social activities, and personal hobbies. Then schedule your work hours using whatever time is left. This goes hand in hand with the famous quote by Benjamin Franklin who once said: "The optimal strategy for high productivity is to split your days into one third work, one third play, and one third rest."

In order to avoid feeling hopeless and stressed-out when all of your tasks crumble up together because of your procrastination you should see prioritizing as a preventive measure in order for this not to happen. See it as something that will ease up your everyday life and duties in ways that you cannot imagine; you must see it as something extraordinary, because it is, and then embrace it and apply to every aspect of your life. Now that you know the huge importance that comes with prioritizing the only logical step for me to follow is to let you know of ways in which you can achieve the ultimate prioritizing skills.

The foundation of time management is that you must prioritize your projects in order to make sure that your working on what is really important rather than on minor things that will end up being major set backs. According to Steve Pavlina of Personal Development for Smart People, "for prioritization to have any meaning, it's imperative that you have a clear objective. For the military your overall objective may be to achieve a decisive victory. Your personal objective may be a set of goals, your mission statement or purpose, or even a state of being. The role of prioritization then is to help you achieve this result with as little effort as possible." So now:

How to Prioritize?

We should begin by recognizing that just because something is good is not a sufficient reason for doing it. As stated in Time Management Guide, "One key reason why prioritizing works, and works well, is the 80/20 Rule. The 80/20 Rule states that 80 percent of our typical activities contribute less than 20 percent to the value of our work." This 80/20 rule is basically saying that even if you leave some of the least important things undone, you would've still have completed most of your work taking the most advantage of your time. "Prioritization is the key to the success of any business or in any walk of life. Being proactive rather than being reactive leads to success." Starting with this self-explanatory quote by time management guru Sean Covey, I will continue using his method of how to prioritize in the best way possible in order to provide you with a series of steps that will guide you in setting your priorities. The first thing you should do is begin with a list of things that you have or should do. After you have your list, which may include things like, writing a paper, taking kids to school, studying for a final, and/or going to the gym you should rate each thing that is in the list in order of importance. You can classify your tasks in the following way:

> Must Do—these goals or activities must be achieved. These are your highest priority goals or activities.
> Should Do—these goals or activities should be achieved (but are not essential)
> Nice to Do (leisure and fun activities)

Following this, I cannot try to teach you on how to prioritize without talking about the urgent/important activity matrix, which was also created by Sean Covey. This matrix is based on all tasks being assigned a level of 'urgency' and 'importance' as illustrated below.

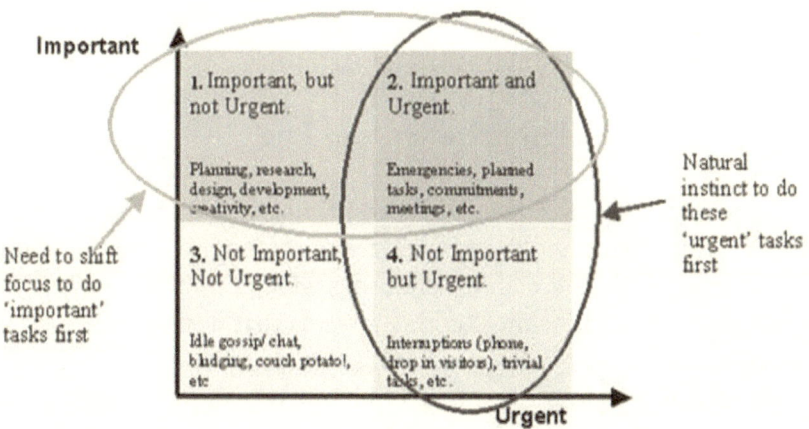

The following steps on how to use the urgent/important activity matrix were taken from Sean Covey's famous book The 7 Habits for Highly Effective People:

➢ The first step is to list all the activities and projects you feel you have to do. Try to include everything that takes up your time at work, however unimportant. (If you manage your time using an Action Program, you'll have done this already.)

➢ Next, assign importance to each of the activities—you can do this on, say, a scale of 1 to 5: remember, this is a measure of how important the activity is in helping you meet your goals and objectives. Try not to worry about urgency at this stage, as this helps get to the true importance.

➢ Once you have assigned importance to each activity, evaluate the urgency of each activity. As you do this, you can plot the listed items on the matrix according to the assigned importance and urgency.

➢ Now study the matrix using the strategies described below to schedule your priorities.

Now that you have a much better understanding of everything that revolves around prioritization, I hope that you will apply it in every aspect of your life and see how it will definitely make it better. By recognizing, organizing, and setting your priorities, you are well on your way to become a highly successful, organized individual who is able to manage his/her time and in this way lives a much better stress-free life.

VIII—B
Prioritization and Life

Everybody has priorities in their lives, either depending on a certain situation or having them as a whole. It is interesting to have the point of view that priorities are about choosing what is more important in a given situation and making actions towards that decision. To have a more broad definition, a reference will be made to an article in which it is stated that priorities is a way of either ranking or putting things in order of importance, that is to say an event or schedules of arrangement that matter most in the scale of things. (Free Encyclopedia, 2011)

During this work, prioritization will be studied and explained not only as one definition, but as a broad concept that includes different types of steps and processes. It will also be reviewed all the ways in which prioritization can be applied depending on the kind of people that is using it. Another issue that may be brought will be about how connected prioritization, motivation, and goals are with one person and with an entire team.

When one talks about priorities the concept of goals may come into the table. This may occur because when a person determines his or her priorities it will motivate them to succeed. According to Joe E. Lawrence in his article "What are priorities and why are they important?" he states that priorities will never define a person, but it will make a person succeed by determining them. It is also explained that once you have found your ultimate goal, priorities is what is going to make you fight for it.

The terms of priorities and goals can be associated together by stating that defining one's priorities is actually a basic step towards achieving one's goal. By following this step, a person can be assured that is moving forward and is getting somewhere instead of being stagnated and getting nowhere. Prioritization is the key to be successful, by only knowing the difference between what is important and what is not.

Now that the concept of priority has been explained and associated with other factors such as goals and decisions, it is important to know how to set them. To define one's goal one must follow steps with basic approaches, which are mainly concerned with planning and making strategies.

According to Donald Martin in his article "How to be successful" he mentions a three-list method to define one's priorities. These methods are divided in: the weekly calendar, the daily "things to do", and goals and other things. In order to utilize this method, first we must understand each one of the steps and how to work with them depending on the given situation.

As first step on the list, there is the weekly calendar, which as it is stated in the article, this concept is about creating a weekly calendar where every activity that one may perform during the day is written in the calendar. It is very important to do first the activities that need more focus and priority in one's life. One must be flexible in adapting the schedule to the priority needs and be able to change it if it doesn't work.

The author of this article refers in this point that is crucial to give the most important activities the exact time they need to be performed and to do them at first. Being able to change everything else in order to deal with priorities is needed in order to fulfill this part of the list. When we focus all our energy into one priority (in this case the activity that is chosen) is when we do our best and the best possible results will come through.

The second step of the list referred in the article is the daily "things to do". In this section it is explained that one must write down all the activities one wants to perform that day without excluding anything. In order to reduce decision making process and disorganization; this list works as a reminder and as a setting for daily priorities. The daily list of "things to do" can be also use to measure one's day-to-day success and in that way one can also check one's sense of accomplishment.

In this step, is impose an idea about measuring the little accomplishments that one may perform each day in order to see how far one is going, or if there is more effort needed to put in action. There is also the statement that by analyzing and measuring our daily activities we are able to achieve more and more without the need of creating major risks or problems that may arise on the way of achieving success.

The third step that is mentioned on the article is goals and other things. In this part the author makes emphasis on the idea that one can make a choice in either making a long-term list or a short-term list. On the list, one must write their goals and the things they need to do to achieve them. The purpose of this list is to learn to develop your own goals and write them down in order to keep a track of the actions perform towards those goals.

As it can be seen the third step relays more on whether a person is a manager or is a leader, because by knowing that one can determine if the list will be short term or long term. In this case, being a leader or being a manager will also determine the size of one's goals and the processes that are going to be use to pursue them. By making the third step, it is guaranteed that less problems will happened in the future because there is more organization when the list is made.

As it can be noted the three-list method is a really good way for measuring a person's progress towards achieving the ultimate goal. It is also an organized method that makes accommodations with the whole direct purpose of prioritizing the most important activities.

It must also be mentioned in this work that prioritization is a way of taking out the best from time and resources available. For this part, a reference will be made to the article "Focus on priorities" from Mind Tools. By understanding the concepts of time and resources, some other issues such as tools, analysis, and processes in prioritization will be explained as well.

According to the article "Focus on priorities", prioritization is the essential skill one need to make the very best use of one's efforts and those of team. In other words, prioritization becomes a distinctive competence that a person may have in using their energy into what is important, and that it can also be taught to other persons. As it can be noted, this article not only refers to the ability of prioritizing itself, but also to the ability of making others understand it and follow the concept.

In the article, prioritization is also referred as a skill that one need to create calmness and space in your life so that one can focus one's energy and attention on the things that really matter. So, as it was stated before, defining priorities is a way of reducing disorganization, wasted time, and activities with weak importance level, by having full focus and concentration over the important activities that are going to make one reach the goal.

The article "Focus on priorities" also states an important managerial or executive point of view which involves time and demand. It refers to the issue that occurs when time is limited and demands are unlimited. By prioritizing, one can allocate time where it is most needed and most wisely spent and that gives freedom from making less important activities that can be attended later. In other words, it is all about knowing which activities will produce better results in order to use the time for them.

The article also makes reference about having a good prioritization or having a bad prioritization as an individual. It states that with a good prioritization one can bring order to chaos, massively reduce stress, and move towards a successful condition, while having a bad prioritization one will flounder around in the unlimited demands. As it is explained in the article, it is very interesting to notice that this statement portrays the sense that it is all about defining priorities at the beginning of everything to have a good work environment. Otherwise, not knowing what the basic priorities are will create disorganization with an excessive amount of wasted time and profit.

Another important concept that is explained in the article "Focus on priorities" is about simple prioritization, which is stated as a way of prioritizing at a simple level that is based on time constraints, on potential profitability, or on the pressure of getting the job done. In other words, this is a process which is fully concentrated on prioritizing considering specific facts brought by the situation and the kind of environment in which it must be performed. For instance, by having a deadline to finish the work one can refer it to pressure, or by knowing that a reward such as getting promoted will come after finishing a specific project, can be consider as potential profitability.

Now that simple prioritization has been explained, emphasis will be made into the concepts that came with it which are: time, profit, and pressure. As it is stated in the article, prioritization based in time constraints is important when other people are depending on one to complete the task that in this case is the critical path of the project. It is also said that in this situation a small amount of one's effort can go a very long way. In other words, prioritization doesn't need to be an entire issue because it can be a very small activity that is the key to complete the process and for others to move on into their activities.

Another concept that is bring into the table is about prioritization being based on project value or profitability, which as it is implied in the article it is the most used and the most common one of all three types. It is explained that this concept gives the most efficient results no matter in what way one may approach it. As it can be noted, usually something that will give a person some kind of reward is the best way to create the kind of incentive that gets the job done in a very efficient way.

And lastly there is also mentioned in the article "Focus on priorities" the third concept about the pressure of getting the job done. The article basically makes reference to the pressure that a boss can eject to its employees in completing a task. It is uncommon to see a person resisting towards his or her boss's mandates in completing a job and that is why it can be set and called as making prioritization. As it can be seen, this concept deals a lot with the environment of work that the employee may be dealing with; whether it is a department filled with pressure from coworkers or whether it is a calmer environment.

After viewing the concept of simple prioritization, the article's content opens the door to other uses of prioritization which would be not considered as simple because it needs the implementation of certain tools into the process. The article "Focus on priorities" mentions the different tools, which are: Paired comparison analysis, Grid analysis, the Action priority matrix, the urgent/important matrix, the Ansoff matrix and the Boston matrices, Pareto analysis, and the Nominal Group technique.

Starting out with the Paired comparison analysis, the article makes reference to the idea that this method is the most useful when decision criteria are vague, subjective, and inconsistent. In other words, this method works is best when the decision-making process is very weak. It is also stated that the Paired comparison analysis helps one to prioritize options by asking oneself to compare items on a list with other items on the same list individually, and then by that deciding which is the most important item on the list. As it can be seen, it is very important to make comparisons to determine which are the exceptional qualities that an item may possess to be prioritize among the others.

The next method that is mentioned in the article is called the Grid analysis, in which it is said that it helps one to prioritize a list of tasks where one needs to take many different factors and resources into account. This process is very useful when one needs to consider other factors such as teamwork and other important activities because it helps one to make the decision of which activity one needs to spend more time in it. For instance, in every process in a company one must always prioritize the bottleneck of the company because from it will depend the whole capacity of the company.

Another method that is explained in the article "Focus on priorities" is the Action Priority Matrix, which is a quick and simple diagramming technique that asks one to plot the value of the task against the effort it will consume. In other words, it is similar as making a graph in which the independent variable will be the value of the task and the dependent variable acts as the effort that the task consumes.

The article also states that by using the Action Priority Matrix one can quickly spot the "quick wins" which are the points that will provide the greatest rewards in the shortest possible time, and it will also spot the "hard logs" which are the ones the soak up time for little reward. As it can be seen, this method will actually provide which exact task will give profit by using little amount of time and which tasks will make one waste time by earning less profit. This method is considered to be an ingenious approach for making prioritization decisions highly efficient.

Now the point have been reached where prioritization's attributes of being urgent or being important may be defined with the approach of the Urgent/Important Matrix given in the article of "Focus on priorities". This technique is found out to be similar to the Action Priority Matrix, but in this one it is ask to think about whether tasks are urgent or important. Usually urgent tasks are not that important in the sense that those activities will not get one to reach the goal, but really important activities are not just that urgent either.

As it is very interesting the concept of urgent and important matrix, now a reference is made to an article called "Using time effectively, not just efficiently", which is provided by Mind Tools. First, it is useful to know the difference between urgent and important activities; as it is stated in the article, an important activity will always have the outcome that leads to the achievement of one's goals. The urgent activities are the ones that demand immediate attention and are usually associated with the achievement of someone else's goals.

Moving on in the context of being important and being urgent, the article posted by Mind Tools also makes a remarkable reference in the concept that is being explained. It is stated that urgent activities are the ones that people concentrate the most because of the critical character they posses at the moment. This activities demand attention and immediate response to them, making one forget about the important activities. This is why the urgent and important matrix becomes a powerful tool for thinking about priorities by making one overcome the tendency of doing urgent activities first instead of the important activities.

The urgent/important matrix is all about measuring the values of the activities in order to determine whether they are urgent or important. To be able to fully understand this concept, in here will be provided a graphical figure of the matrix where it can be seen the level of significance that each activity must be measured on. This figure was also obtained from the article "Using time effectively, not just efficiently" from Mind Tools.

Figure 1: Urgent/Important Matrix

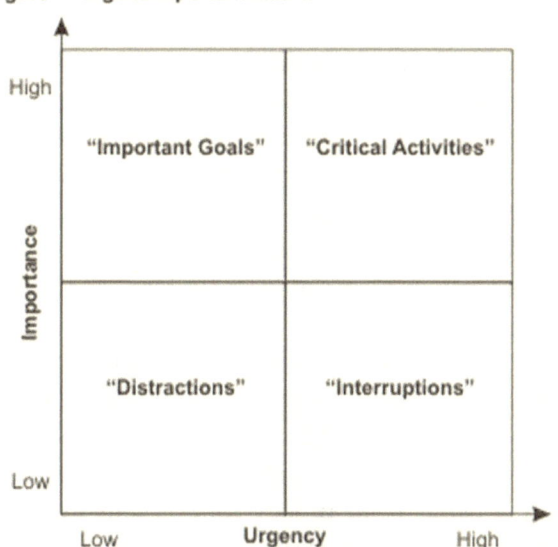

Now that the concept of Urgent/Important Matrix has been extensively explained, the work can move on into the next method of the Ansoff Matrix and the Boston Matrices, which is provided in the article of "Focus in priorities". This method has been proved to be a good technique for prioritizing the opportunities that come to one. The Ansoff Matrix helps one to evaluate and measure opportunities by risks; while the Boston Matrix helps one to prioritize opportunities based on market attributes and the ability that one possess to take advantage of that market. As it can be noted, both of these matrices evaluate opportunities given with factors that deal with the ability of the person of identifying risks and studying the markets.

The next method that is going to be viewed from the article is the Pareto Analysis. As it is stated in the article this method is needed when one is facing a big array of problems needing to be solve, because the Pareto Analysis will help one identify which are the most important changes needed to be made. This technique first works by asking the person to group the problems together and then count the number of cases in each problem. By doing this, one is prioritizing the most common type of problem so that the person can focus his or her efforts in resolving it and by that creating more time to resolve other problems. In other words, this method helps one to take out the problems that happen more often to regroup them so that time can be managed more effectively.

And last but not least, the article mentions the method of Nominal Group Technique, which is a useful technique for prioritizing issued and projects within a group, by giving every person a fair input into the prioritization process. In other words, this process works by giving individuals the same value of contribution into the prioritization system by working as a team. This concept is taken into action when many opinions about a subject is given, and when many decisions have to be made.

In the article "Focus on priorities", it is explained that when using the Nominal Group Technique each member of the group nominates the priority issue that he or she thinks is more important and then a scale is created to rank them. It is mainly noticed from this method the fairness that acts beneath the process for everyone to be able to express their opinion and make choices together as a group.

As it can be seen, there are many ways in which prioritization can be used either in the business world or for personal situations. The most important thing is to first know and define which the situations that one is dealing with and whether one must prioritize as a team or individually. And then it is important to also know if one is defining and measuring priorities according to scales or standards set.

One thing that was found very interesting is that at the end of every article reviewed on this work, it was noticed that the article provides the reader with other electronically direction in which one can take tests or buy books or learn techniques to actually acquire the skill of prioritization. This made one think that prioritization is something that can be learn if one does not possess it as an innate characteristic. Either way, the important issue to understand is that being a leader or being a manager in this case will not create restrictions to any of them because both may have this skill.

Another thing that is also important to make emphasis on is that after researching and learning about priorities one is not only getting knowledge about it, but is also acquiring the ability of getting an immediate response in knowing where prioritization is needed. In conclusion, one can learn that priorities does not always have to be chosen from an obvious and probabilistic point of view, because it is something that can be found out by following simple steps. It must also be mention that when a person sets his or her own priorities is having an start and an advantage in every process that the person may perform.

"Always bear in mind that your own resolution to succeed is more important than any other"

Abraham Lincoln

CHAPTER IX

Staffing

Nowadays we face, as young businessman, the challenge of entering in a ferocious competitive globalized market with still raw or not so refined ideas and experience that would help and back up us in certain situations. Its obvious that in order to get these ideas transformed into a lucrative project, we need to build a team, which would let us attack more effectively future challenges. This is why we need a workforce, which would support you to reach your goals and accomplish what proposed. In order to correctly build a strong foundation in our growing business, we need to develop and apply good staffing and training strategies. In other words, this would be one of our first matters to be taken into account in a starting business. Creating a ferocious and effective workforce by developing strong methods for staffing and training our future personal. strategies.

We should now focus in the staffing process, which would be our very first step in creating our business's foundation. Staffing can be better referred or known as recruitment.

Recruitment refers to the process of attracting, screening, and selecting qualified people for a specified job. Recruitment-related functions are generally carried out by an organization's human resources staff. The stages in recruitment include sourcing candidates by advertising, screening potential candidates using tests and/or interviews, selecting candidates based the the results of the tests and/

or interviews, and on-boarding to ensure the candidate is able to fulfill their new role effectively.

Our recruitment process should follow the following steps (2):

1. **Job Analysis**
   - A recruitment effort starts by performing a job analysis, to document the actual or intended requirement of the job to be performed. This information is captured in a job description and provides the recruitment effort with the boundaries and objectives of the search. Starting a recruitment with an accurate job analysis and job description ensures the recruitment effort starts off on a proper track for success.

2. **Sourcing**
   - We should start an advertising campaign, encompassing multiple media, such as the Internet, general newspapers, job ad newspapers, professional publications, window advertisements, job centers, and campus graduate recruitment programs.
   - Conduct a recruiting research, which would led to the proactive identification of relevant talent who may not respond to job postings and other recruitment advertising methods done in the job analysis. This research is also called name-generation, and give results to a list of prospects who can then be contacted to solicit interest, obtain a resume/CV, and be screened.

3. **Screening & Selection**
   - We now should proceed in looking for skills which would define the suitability for a job. Skills in skills communication, typing, and computer skills should be proficient. Qualifications may be shown through the process of revising resumes, job application and performing interviews, looking for educational or professional experience, and references. Other resume screening criteria may include length of service, job titles and length of time at a job.

4. Onboarding
- We should now proceed to develop a process of helping new employees become productive members of an organization. A well planned introduction helps new employees become fully operational quickly and is often integrated with a new company and environment.

After the staffing process is finished, the training of the already in force personal is due. This process refers to the acquisition of knowledge, skills, and competencies as a result of the teaching of vocational or practical skills and knowledge that relate to specific useful competencies. Training solidifies the core of apprenticeships and provides the backbone a strong business by improving one's capability, capacity, and performance.

According to Knol specialists, there is an easy five step model you can follow to help you build new training or modify old training to make it objective and effective for your learners:

1. Rationale
- Define why you are conducting the training. Determine the need and be able to state what the benefit of the training is to the learners.

2. Objectives
- Tell your learners what they are about to learn in concrete, verifiable terms.
  Make sure the objectives are actionable and measurable.

3. Activities
- Have them do what you want them to learn. Create opportunities for your learners to practice what they are learning.

4. Evaluating
- Ask them questions and/or have them demonstrate what you are teaching them.

5. **Feedback**
   - Confirm or correct the learner's work. If your learner's work is correct, acknowledge their accomplishment. If they are incorrect, help them see where they made their mistake and offer guidance.

In conclusion, the staffing and training process should be a proactive process, because these processes are the foundations for creating and ensuring a strong team within your business, which will ensure a compete in the ferocious globalized market.

CHAPTER X

Delegation

One of the 10 different managerial skills that could define a good manager from a bad manager is delegation. The fundamental about delegation is about giving the responsibility and entrusting your authority to others in order to accomplish a task successfully and effectively. In other words, is about accomplishing the work through people. As an individual we can only accomplish a limited amount of task in a given time. If we work alone, pressure and workload will increase. This in turn will make us feel stressed, unhappy, and the feeling that we are letting people down. In a business, we need the help from others in order to manage the increase workload in a limited amount of time. Moreover, delegating and completing tasks will help expand the value that we deliver to the business and customers.

Improving this managerial skill will help the business improve the distinctive competence and as person you will be able to achieve more success, by bringing value and gaining experience to take higher responsibilities. "Good delegation saves you time, develops people, grooms a successor, and motivates. Poor delegation will cause you frustration, demotivates and confuses other person, and fails to achieve the task or purpose itself." (Businessballs).

"Delegation underpins a style of management which allows your staff to use and develop their skills and knowledge to the full potential. Without delegation, you lose their full value." (Blair). If workers stay idle there will be negative effects. The company will not be able to accomplish their objectives in time. And the person may lose or forget their skills, which will make them useless for the company. Entrusting your authority to others is what a manager has to risk. They have to take full responsibility whether the task was accomplished successfully or badly.

This responsibility will trigger the workers to be more proactive and independent. However this is not easily accomplished if the managers are not able to use their other managerial skills, like innovation. If we are able to motivate the people and successfully delegate; "the staff will have the authority to react to situations without referring back to you" (Blair). They will be able to develop new skills that will in turn help accomplish a task and be independent. Furthermore, it is important to keep the people learning and improving by each task. "Delegating to a subordinate may be time consuming as you guide and monitor them, but in the end you will save time and frustration as you gain increasingly competent and invested employees who can relieve you of duties that don't require your expertise." (Mulberry).

Communication and information is clearly the main factor in delegation. The manager must be able to communicate accurately the task and information that the workers will need. In order to have a successful delegation, "the workers should have full and rapid access to relevant information in order to make decisions on their own. They must be able to communicate with their partners so they can be aware of what the others are doing" (Blair). Because of this freedom of information access, some managers believe that the workers will use this information for bad purposes, like to rise up, challenge the managers and take control. If we have this mentality, we will not be confident at the time when we delegate. Delegating is about giving responsibilities and be able to trust on others. The managers must be able to use the experience and the knowledge from the staff in order to bring new ideas.

In order to assure that the worker are able to accomplish the tasks; we must be able to know if they are confident enough and if they are capable. The key to successful delegation is to delegate gradually. "If we present a project that is difficult and the staff knows that they are not able to cope, then the task will not be completed and the staff will be demotivated" (Blair). As a manager, we must know the skill limit of our staff. We must be able to give them task that they can accomplish by themselves. As result, they can develop their skills and build confidence in order to do other task. In order to build the confidence we must give them support. For example, they must convince and motivate them that they are capable of completing the task and that there are people willing to help them.

Delegating is not as simple as giving some orders. Delegation also involves processes that must be followed in order to be done successfully. Some of the guideline for successful delegation is: "Define the task, Select the individual, State required result, Support and communicate, Feedback on results" (Businessballs). This guideline will help you delegate better with your subordinates and at the same time, keeping track that everything is done correctly.

Our first step is to define the task. What we want to accomplish, what is our goals. We have to determine if the task to be done is suitable to be delegated.

Certainly tasks that don't require a manager's level of skill or those that require an expertise that the manager doesn't have are among those that can be considered for reassignment. In an ideal situation, the things that a manager delegates to employees should motivate or teach them. (Mulberry)

The tasks that are to be delegated should be challenging and help the people learn and always keep them developing their skills. If the task are not challenging and are routine, people will not be motivated to finish the task or even care if it was done correctly. Since, "boredom can be a destructive force at work" (Mulberry). The assignment should be fun for them and let them cooperate with others so it can be finished effectively and smoothly. "Any task or assignment that is delegated to someone else should be specific in its scope and something that the two can measure so that you know when it is completed, and how successfully it was done" (Mulberry). However, some tasks are not suitable to be delegated. Tasks that involve delicate information and involve decisions that may affect the business in the long run should be analyzed before we assign them to someone. As a manager, deciding what to delegate will help us organize our tasks and know what are being done and how it is done.

The next step is to know who is going to do the task. Who we should give them this responsibility? Should we trust them? Why we chose them? These are some of the questions that a manager should ask himself before handling a task to someone. Before handling the task to others, we should consider the time constraint that they have. "Crushing an employee with an unreasonable expectation will assure failure of the project and probably destroy the employee's morale" (Mulberry). So we have to be careful, we don't want to lower their productivity, we want them to be efficient for us. Next we should consider the abilities and skills that they can offer. We should know if the people are capable and trustworthy, before giving them the task. It is important that they know the responsibility that we are entrusting them. Some of the factors that we should consider when we are delegating to someone are: "The experience, knowledge, and skills of the individual, the individual work style, the workload that this person can handle" (MindTools).

The next step is to state the results, the results that we are expecting. When we delegate, it is important to clarify what we want from our employees and what are the goals that we are seeking. In this way, we can measure the success and keep track of the progress. Moreover, it will be easier to determine who will be assigned for the project and how the task will be done. "The supervisor must discuss exactly what they are asking the employee to take on, what the scope of the assignment is, and why it's critical. It should also be made clear what they will gain by taking on this work" (Mulberry). Stating the results that we expect will help us identify all the resources that we need and the constraint that we will have. Furthermore, it is important to let the employee know that they will have the responsibility to achieve the results that we are looking for.

Moreover, the way we delegate is a factor that will determine if we succeed on a task. The purpose of delegating is to keep always the morale

After planning and stating the results, we should have support and communication. In this stage, we must let everyone know how things are going and how is the progress of the objective. Having a good communication will help the people understand what you are seeking. At the same time, you should be able to state what you want and motivate them. People don't know everything and if we want things to be done correctly, they should know that we are available to help and support them. If problems rises and they are losing track, as a manager we should give them advice and assistance in order to solve this problems. Keeping track on the work will help avoid any problem; however it will look bad if they think we are monitoring every move that they do. They will feel that we don't trust them. In order to solve this, it will be better to ask for a weekly report.

Our last step for delegating is to keep in contact and feedback on results. In this last step, we should let others know if things were done correctly and if the objective was achieved. If the assignment fails, we should still keep in contact and review what was wrong and what the problems occur that didn't let us complete the task. As a manager, we are responsible if things success or fail. That's why we need feedback from the two so next times it could be done better. Practicing feedback also involve constructive criticism. If our employees have problems, we should be able to advise them and help them learn something new, always having immediate response that will be useful for both.

The advantage of practicing this is that we help people grow and develop their knowledge, skills and abilities. This brings value to the company and to our customers.

But just as delegating has grown more difficult, it's also become more crucial for companies seeking to compete. In Covey's words, "Twenty or thirty years ago, only 30 percent of the value added to goods and services came from knowledge work. Now it's 80 percent. So if companies hope to survive, they must empower people to think for themselves and draw on their experience and wisdom. (Johnson)

If we develop people and make them skilled, they become a valuable asset for us. They will be efficient and proactive. Bringing a new employee will be costly; we will need to spend time and money for training. Moreover, they will not be prepared if we assign them a task. They will be more likely to make mistakes.

Now we should address why some managers tend to resist delegations. One of the fears for them is that employees can challenge them and take control. "Some subordinate cannot handle delegated authority because they use it to become abusive with others or even try to challenge their superiors" (Tyson). Moreover, "people don't delegate because it takes a lot of up-front effort" (MindTools). As a manager, you will likely do everything since it is easier for you. And you wouldn't choose someone else since you believe they will make a mistake. We think we can do it better and faster without spending much time. Moreover, it will be faster if you do it by yourself, compared to teaching someone else how to do it. Moreover, we risk that the project will not be finished or will not be done properly. Using a tactical mindset, you will surely complete things faster and will have short term results. But, you will not exactly know what results or achievement you want to accomplish.

However this vision is wrong, you will make best use of your time if you cooperate and work with others. Using a strategic mindset will help you avoid mistakes and failure in the future. "Delegation is mostly used for projects that are large, complex and too fast changing for any one individual. Assigning work to others is an integral part of getting things done efficiently." (MindTools). You will get new ideas and develop the people's skills and abilities in a progressive way. For a future projects, it will be easier to delegate with your employees, because you will have a sense of trust and know the limit of the skills that each person has. We will have better time management, and avoid any frustration or stress caused by unfinished work.

There are three characteristics that we have to take into account when we are handling responsibilities. "These are knowledge and skills, workload and reliability" (Montgomery). First we have to know the skills and knowledge of the people. Whether, the workers are capable of achieving the goals in an efficient way. "It doesn't matter how experienced they are if they don't have the required skills, they will be worthless for us" (Montgomery). For example, if the toilet broke we need a plumber; we don't need a policeman or a firefighter to help us.

The second characteristic that we have to take into account from our workers is the amount of workload that they are capable of handling in the limited amount of time. We should know the limits of each person. If we pass those limits and exhaust them, the productivity will reduce and they will not be motivated to keep working. "Delegating more tasks to them will create additional stress and may decrease the quality of their work. Overworked team members tend to be less creative and more careless" (Montgomery). If we want them to be better, we need to arrange a schedule or be better at time management.

The third characteristic is reliability, the degree of trust and dependability that we give to someone. For the work to be done, we depend on the others. We need to make sure that they comply with what they say. Also, we must know the strength of each person so we can assign them the right task. "Delegating tasks outside of a candidate's most successful work situations will make them much less reliable in completing the tasks within the given parameters. To effectively delegate, work to your team members' strengths" (Montgomery).

As I have mentioned before, the essential for good delegation is the ability to have good communication and the ability to motivate and develop people. As a manager, we deal with objective and task, how they are accomplished. Furthermore, we should exercise interpersonal skills since we deal with people. Delegating help accomplish more work than we could have done as an individual. The decisions that a manager have to take in order to delegate better is to identify the appropriate task to be delegated, plan carefully, monitor, and assure the success of the assignment.

Hence, I will mention some of the primary advantages and disadvantages of delegation. The greatest advantage of delegation is to have the time to do more in a limited amount of time. We will be able to motivate people and increase the self-esteem. Also they will be able to grow and develop new skills. Delegating with different people will help bring new ideas and different solutions for a task that will help improve the company.

Some of the primary disadvantage of delegating is about trust and motivation. Some of the employees will not be fully motivated about the work. They will just tend to finish the work, but they will not give some follow up or input any "extras" from them. Some of the people are not fully skilled and sometimes we can't trust them a lot. They might use inefficiently the resources of time and money. Moreover, they might abuse their authority. That's why before delegating we must know with who we are working, since we have to rely on them.

X—A
The Whats and Hows of Delegating

As managers and leaders of a company a person must be able to carry out many tasks and, as such, must possess many skills. These skills work in correlation with each other and support each other so that there is an overall improvement. Nevertheless, many people believe that these skills are sought individually and must be developed individually or that they are as simple as their definition portrays them to be. Also, not many people are aware of what goes on behind the scenes with these skills nor how and when to use them even when understanding the full extent of these is crucial to the proper development of one's company and determines the success of a person as a leader or manager.

Throughout this paper, you will first learn what to do before you delegate and why people delegate in the first place. Then, there will be a stressed mention on the difference between what is thought to be delegating versus what delegating should be viewed as. Also, the skill of delegating will be addressed along with the necessary aptitudes needed to develop it appropriately and a detailed description of how to handle the art of delegating with the steps that are required in order to go through this process. Finally, to put the cherry on the top, there will be mention of what has to be delegated and a simple view of what has to be done after one learns to delegate appropriately.

Many people that find delegating complicated because of issues of trust or just because they feel they can do things better and by themselves decide at one point that they will simply not delegate and do things by themselves. However this is not feasible and can cause many problems because you are only one person and can do only so many things in a given amount of time. In the end, even "super-you" needs help and support to get the work around the place done; and delegating does just that: It helps you help yourself. You help yourself because as you go through the process to train your employees you gain the trust of the people and allot more time to yourself in order to get started on other aspects of the business and exponentially increase your chances of success[1].

As a key point, it is important to understand that delegating is not just telling people what to do and letting them go to do the task. Delegating is part of a huge process. It is a right that you, as a manager or leader, have to strive to earn. This means that to get to the point where you can tell people what to do and expect the things to be done right and effectively you have to work for it and go through the steps. Moreover, to get to this point, you must understand the people you are working with and you must have the ability to effectively train them in order to make them competent in what they are doing for you. But above all, one must realize that delegating is a two-way street it isn't something you do to people but something that you do with people[2].

However, before you delegate, or even start on the process, you must first plan. As a manager, you have to plan and decide the tasks to delegate, since your time as manager is cut out for you and brings a lot of value to the company. To do this, you can start out by making a list of the things that you do every day and decide what things you can assign to your subordinates. This step is needed in order for you to liberate yourself from everyday not-so-important responsibilities that your people can do fairly well for you. The best thing is that by doing this you can multiply yourself through your employees and the business can continue to operate even if you are not around[3].

Getting into what we need, delegation requires a clear understanding of people in terms of their competence and commitment. These two aspects of an employee make up what is the employee's, and therefore also the company's, intellectual capital. This type of capital is the most important of all to the company as it is capital that does not depreciate and whose demand in the workplace is increasing[4]. To be clearer on the matter, we find that competence, in this equation, is not the same as ability. Competence is dexterity in certain tasks that can be developed and taught in order to be increased; while ability is something useful that is simply natural to the person, something that the person intuitively does well. And commitment is simply that little push that keeps you doing what you have to do. It is determined by confidence and the amount of motivation or inspiration that a person has in the matter. Both of these aspects when considered together determine how developed a person becomes. Bear in mind, however, that having only one of these can prove disastrous for the company. For example, a person that enters a company might be very committed because he is excited, but if he has no competence in the matter he would end up being perceived as troublesome rather than helpful since he doesn't really know what he is doing and could end up making a complete mess of things.

Being good at delegating, also requires an acknowledgment of the huge differences that exist among people and as such requires the manager or leader to be flexible in approaching each person individually. Not only that but, as a manager, one must also realize when a person is changing and must, at that time as well, change his approach of working with that person so as to yield the most rewarding outcomes from the situation. To do this a manager or leader should be very aware of the situation around him and must develop the right judgment in order to know when to let go of a certain approach and at the same time requires that one be proactive in the ability of training those people that are working with him or her.

Getting into the meat of the matter, a person that delegates must have organizational skills as well in order to know which approach to use with each person. This means that the person that delegates must know what task a person is good at and how well this person can handle each task. Knowing this, a manager can figure out whether to delegate work or responsibility to people. This makes a huge difference for the fact that delegating work is a more directive approach telling the person what to do and what not to, as well as telling them how to do it. On the other hand, delegating a responsibility requires that you let go of the person and trust them to do something by themselves, pitching in that bit of support when they get start to lose motivation. As such, we find that delegating responsibilities is a more supportive way of delegating.

Going on defining these characteristics of delegating we can finally define the different approaches that we have been talking so much about. Mixing in directive and supportive behaviors we come up with four management styles: 1) Directing, 2) Coaching, 3) Supporting and 4) Delegating[5]. All these approaches provide a mix of the direction and support and each subsequent level is less time consuming for a manager. As such, a manger will ideally want to be spending less time with each employee and have time to think about more strategic matters. But this is easier said than done, as a long process is required in order to move from each style to the next and the manager needs to be extremely flexible in the sense that he or she must be able to handle all these styles at the same time with different people, and if needed for the same person in different activities. It sounds complicated and it really is. It requires dedication and understanding, an understanding of what each of these approaches or style refer to specifically and why they yield results in a working environment.

Let's start off with directing. Directing requires that a manager dictate with his orders. The manager must tell the people what to do and how and provides a clear definition of what is right and wrong. In this case, the employee is being sort of controlled in the sense that the employee is not being allowed to think for himself but is rather being told what to do. This style works well when the people you are working with are very committed but not very competent. You see, your employees in this case will not mind the bossing around because their motivation has them excited and they don't mind doing anything.

At the same time the clear portrayal of what to do and how to do it develops the person's competence and as such the person starts to develop skills that are more useful for the company.

As you go on working with this employee, he or she will start losing commitment or inspiration to do the tasks that you assign. This loss of commitment arises from the fact that sometimes tasks turn out to be more difficult than what was expected, or simply because the employee has had enough of bossing around. In this case, you must move on and start to use a coaching style. This style, gives the employee some support and a lot of direction. In other words you make the employee feel more involved in what he or she is doing. You must tell him or her things like: we have so and so problem and I would like to know what you feel we should do about it. In a sense, you introduce you employee to decision-making and start to guide instead of dictating.

As the person receives support, his commitment which has been on the fall starts to rise again and he feels like he can do more, however it is important not to let this person completely off the leash as he still has a lot to learn in order to develop the necessary skills in order to be productive for the company. It is also important to know when to switch over from a directive to a coaching style because if you switch to early over to a coaching style you have wasted a time span that you could have used in order to complement the employee's working skills and in the very near future the type of support that you provide will have diminished effect on a unmotivated employee.

The next step to a delegating style is to be supportive. The employee, by now, must have learned the skills needed to work and knows exactly what he or she has to do. Nevertheless, their motivation to work is of a varying nature because confidence becomes a major issue in this situation. This is due to the fact that as you slowly let go of the person he will, in more times than one, find him/herself in a situation where insecurity pops in and he doesn't have the floor that assured him that he was on the right track. So, at this point you must fend to boost the confidence of your employee. You start making major decisions along with your employee and you start facilitating the efforts that your employee has in mind. You must encourage and give the awaited thumbs up to your employees in order to keep them up, running and confident of the fact that they are on the right path. As mentioned before, the employee will have no need of being told what to do since he or she already knows that from the skills that were learned in the past and the leadership skill that boosted his or her competence in matters of work.

However, before you switch over to a supportive style of delegating, you must absolutely make sure that the person knows what he is doing. You see, leaving a person alone while giving them all the confidence in the world can lead to their own demise which will come from an overconfidence that will have arisen from being supported so much, even though they aren't really competent. Also, you must make sure that you can trust the person to do the job in the given amount of time, because here you are handing over a responsibility not just work. This is said because, there is no point in giving the work to a competent person if this person needs to be constantly triggered in order to do his job (this case would suit a coaching style approach as his motivation to work is still very low).

You must keep supporting this person until you find that he can handle her/himself. At this point in time you can turn in complete responsibility for decision-making and problem solving to the employee. As may be seen, the role of the manager here is minimal and therefore this is what managers aim for so that they may handle more relevant aspects of the company. However, many people feel that this is absolutely everything that managers do; they feel that managers just abdicate work with no worries even if this isn't true at all—at least for a good manager.

At this point, where your employee can handle himself, you have just knocked upon the doors of delegation. While delegating, your employee finds motivation in himself and has already been trained in order to have the competence needed at work. As such, he is a self-made employee (or at least he thinks he is) that gets inspiration from doing things right and knowing that he is growing in the process. The manager, however, implementing a delegating style must never leave the employee completely alone and must, at least once in a while, pop by to check how things are going in matters such as: if the employee is as enthusiastic as ever and is doing his work in line with the imbibed values and goals in mind. It is then at this point, when a person feels he did it by himself or herself, that a manager has covered the whole process in order to truly delegate such an employee.

Another important thing to add is that while going through the steps there must be a good communication between you and the employee.

This is because these styles require sudden changes in behavior with the employee being discussed and as such could leave the employee in doubt and wasting energy thinking about things that are not. For example, say you support someone all along with a supportive style and then decide it's time to delegate this person. You will meet this person less since you are confident that he will carry out the job well; however, the employee will still seek that support from you as it is of custom. So, it is important to explain to the employee how you will be changing your behavior so that he or she may be prepared. In this scenario, telling the employee that you will be giving him more freedom than before because of his given feats and accomplishments will rather assure that he will find motivation in his work and himself.

As we now know how to get to what actually is delegating and how to go through the steps, we must also realize that it doesn't all end here. You see, a manager's job isn't at all to just abdicate, or give out work and simply expect the things to happen just as he or she said. A manager must also make sure that what he says is being done or if things are going smoothly. For such reasons, a manager must know how to supervise appropriately. However, before he supervises he must make sure that he has clearly defined what purpose or objectives he expects from his employee so as to be able to measure the improvement and to truly know when he can shift his employees through the different steps that lead on to delegating.

While setting goals for an employee many managers nowadays tend to use the SMART method. SMART is an acronym for Specific, Measurable, Achievable, Realistic and Time-Bound[6]. This as a whole points out that a manager must make sure that he is not confusing or frustrating the employee beyond his capacity. That is to say that a manager must reduce the goals and objectives to about 3-5 in order for there to be a clear and specific picture on the matter. It is important here to note that each objective must have a given time frame in order to know when it is expected to have completed this task. This is to keep a steady amount of pressure on the employee as well as to be able to measure them appropriately in matters of timeliness and efficiency. Also, as a manager you must make sure that all the objectives are realistic and achievable since an impossible goal will not only be out of grasp for the employee in the given time frame, but will also snatch away motivation from the employee and get him to work in a discouraged manner.

As you have your goals set and trust your employee to the point that you only need to get back with him or her once in a while to see how things are going it is smooth sailing from there. However, it is important not to trust in your employee too much as well. There are certain tasks that as a manager you must carry out yourself at all times. According to the Harvard ManageMentor, for example, you should retain responsibility for things such as: planning directing and motivating your team; performance evaluations; complex negotiations; hiring, firing and career development[7]. To this list we could even add things such as capital and financial decisions and risk management decisions. In short, anything that has to do anything with high risks for the company and things directly related to other employees to eliminate the possibility of favoritism or grudges taking place in the company.

All in all what we must learn is that delegating is not just one skill that a manager must master, but it is a necessity for him or her if he doesn't want to end up doing everything himself and end up frustrated. Also, delegating is not a solitary deal. It comes with a whole web of interconnected activities that enhance it and enable a manager, once he understands its true meaning, to carry it out as he should. In turn, he must also use it to train his employees and be able to carry out the functions of the company more efficiently than he could ever do by himself.

Once a manager has decided to delegate, has planned what to delegate, and has gotten over the problems of trust and the fear of handing out responsibilities, he must start straight out and attend to his employees. He must provide what is lacking in them in terms of competence and commitment using his organizational skills and must be highly flexible in his approach in order to tend to each employee as he or she changes and to be able to deal with different employees all together. However, he must not forget to keep them communicated as he works with them using a combination of directive and supportive styles and starts switching between them.

As a delegation becomes inherent to a manager he must also realize that he must supervise what he delegates as per the strategy he is using (less supervision for the more supportive styles) because it is only then that he can really know if things are being done well. To facilitate supervision managers must set SMART objectives that allow them to have clear goals set for their employees that can be easily measured and, therefore, supervised. Furthermore, as a manager one must also realize that not everything is capable of being delegated and that certain tasks should be left to the disposition of the manager—these tasks including those dealing with the relationship of other employees to the company, as well as capital and high risk decisions that deal with the company's resources.

In the end, if all is done well, delegation will prove very fruitful to the company and the manager. This is mainly for delegation "frees up the top person to do their strategic thinking and make sure the big picture's being addressed[8]." And when the big picture is being addressed a manager knows what is coming, prepares himself for what is coming, and is capable of taking problems head on in order to keep growing and pocketing success.

CHAPTER XI

Supervising

The business dictionary states that supervising is the process of monitoring and regulating of processes, or delegated activities, responsibilities, or tasks. In the work place, the one who supervises is known as the supervisor. Supervisors have to monitor the activities that are in progress to make sure they are done right and on time, and that the objects and targets are reached. They are also responsible for the productivity and progress in an organization. Supervising, is overseeing the progress and productivity of direct reports and of activities performed in their area of work.

A supervisor is a high management position where the basic management skills have to be applied in order to keep the business going. Some of these skills include: delegating, staffing and training, prioritizing, organizing, and planning. But most important they must have the working knowledge of the activities being performed in their group.

Delegating is a good way to build trust from the supervisor to the employees. This in turn provides you with more time to oversee the organizations' operations. In order to properly delegate a supervisor must have effective communication skills and provide a positive work environment, so that employees know what they need to do and feel good about their work and effort put fourth on their work.

To supervise or supervision of a group of employees includes:

1. Conducting basic management skills (decision making, problem solving, planning, delegation and meeting management)

2. Organizing their department and teams
3. Noticing the need for and designing new job roles in the group
4. Hiring new employees
5. Training new employees
6. Employee performance management (setting goals, observing and giving feedback, addressing performance issues, firing employees, etc.)
7. Conforming to personnel policies and other internal regulations

A supervisor should always be present in an organization or company. If the organization is big enough, the supervisor will have a Human Resource Department, which will support and direct the supervisors' activities. "They will also guide and support activities in staffing, development and management of personnel policies and records, training and development, performance appraisals and performance problems, career counseling, organization development, etc. HR provides this help and ensures that all activities conform to current rules and regulations."

Even though there exists the possibility of having a Human Resource department, the supervisor is still responsible of ensuring that employees follow the organization's policies and procedures. They must also make sure that the needs of the employees are met, and consequently the supervisor is usually the first to notice the need of new/more employees. They must go over resumes and conduct the actual interview. Since the supervisor is the one who is or should be capable to know what is going on in the organization, he is the one who can recommend who should be hired from other candidates and what is the best position that person is perfect for.

As soon as the new employee begins working, the supervisor is responsible for orienting the employee through the organizations, and providing guidance like counseling and coaching. By doing this, a supervisor can help the employee fulfill his/her career goals, so that they reach their own goals and as consequence the organizations' as well. By guiding the employees, they must set performance standards for the different tasks, jobs and roles of their employees. As employees advance in their work, feedback about their performance should be provided. With this feedback, they will be able to see how they are doing in their job and in what areas they should improve.

Supervising also involves coaching employees. Supervisors must work with their employees to establish goals, action plans and time lines. "The supervisor delegates and also provides ongoing guidance and support to the employee as they complete their action plans. Rarely can job goals be established without considering other aspects of an employee's life, e.g., time available for training, career preferences, personal strengths and weaknesses, etc."

Overseeing the performance of the organization and of individual employees gives supervisors a unique vision of the employees and their job and career advancement. This is why the employees sometimes see them as mentors. They become a model for direction and growth.

In order to successfully supervise, you must identify your personal opportunities for growth and education, and as already mentioned you must also help your employees succeed and grow within the organization. I think that you must first know who you are and not try to be someone you're not. Be yourself and in doing so use your own style of managing-supervising skills, ideas and practices.

I believe it is important to always be open-minded and learn from previous managers and mentors who have helped you be who you are and where you are. Try to also be a role model for your employees. They are always looking at the supervisor for approval and acceptance. "You need to set the bar and make sure that they know where it is set and what your expectations are of them." As a coach, mentor and supervisor you must have the ability to build trust and earn your employees respect. Employees need to know you are there when they need you and in turn they should be there for you as well.

CHAPTER XII

Measuring

How important is to measure everything in businesses.

"When you can measure what you are speaking about, and express it in numbers, you know something about it; but when you cannot measure it, when you cannot express it in numbers, your knowledge is of a meager and unsatisfactory kind . . ." One thing that one should always measure is the performance of the business. This will keep one focused on the advantages and disadvantages, and the strengths and the weaknesses in ones business. When one knows where to center the attention, one is able to apply any solving method and base on what ones measure, one is able to do some decision making, improvement, updates, or changes so that one's business has less risk or reduce weakness or disadvantages. It is very important that one is always measuring the risks or things like the financial ratios. If one is always taking in consideration everything that can go wrong one is able to be more close to the objective and to the best business performance.

One thing that is vital is that after measuring things in businesses, is that one should take action to always improve so that the business is always growing in a positive way. Usually this is what is call an strategic business plan, which help one to focus on the different type of activities that are more significant for ones business. As I already mention, it is recommended to update every time ones business have change its goals or important things to develop. It is also suggested that one should be recording everything so that one is able to look back to the things that were measure before and how things react.

The problem comes when ones do not know what to measure and you do the measures but not the relevant are been study. The results of these wrong measures are that any change, update, improvement will not be positive to ones business. So it is primordial to measure the correct things so one is able to make the correct decision or to know that one is going the correct path.

The following points have been found in "Balanced Scorecard Institute" Combining elements of various measurement frameworks yields the measurement model below. It works as follows:

1. The needs and expectations of customers and stakeholders are the primary drivers of strategies. Stakeholders include shareholders and employees, but suppliers, the community, government entities and other organizations could also be important stakeholders.

2. Strategy consists of defining your intended customers and how you are going to compete for them. A company's strategy is made up of individual strategies, which are the key actions a company must take to achieve its vision and goals. When developing strategies, all other elements of the model must be considered.

3. Operations include all direct and support business activities that execute strategies and produce products and services for customers and stakeholders.

4. The capabilities of a company's organization and infrastructure enable its operations to efficiently satisfy customer and stakeholder requirements. Stakeholder capabilities may also be important to a company's operations. In the short-term, capabilities can limit what strategies are feasible; in the long-term they may need to be developed to implement certain strategies.

5. Stakeholder contributions include products or services that are essential to operations. For example, suppliers may provide critical technical support for designing products.

6. Products and services provided to customers create financial returns (7) for shareholders and perhaps other stakeholders as well.

CHAPTER XIII

Reporting

The Importance of Reporting from a Managerial point of view

The act of reporting is one in which we tell someone about a certain topic, we inform the person. We almost always use reporting in our day to day life. When our boss asks us about someone's task or how he's doing at work we are reporting. Even when your mom asks you how your sister behaved you are reporting. We are always using different opinions on properness value in reporting. It is very important for you and for the person who is listening to you, that the report is worth of hearing, reading or seeing. We must know that the clarity of the information is the core of reporting. Reporting can be divided into two large groups the formal and informal reports. Along with the different types of reports in which to develop, we must also be aware of what it means to do a good report and the different styles it compiles. When we look at articles, books, or internet, we see plenty of reporting styles and forms.

When preparing a report we must know that after choosing the type of report and what style of report we are doing we must focus on the story that is being covered. We should ask ourselves questions like, Is the report clear enough and easy to be understood? Could it be clarified? Is it an honest report? Clear and easy to understand are very important in reporting. Its all about effectiveness, that why the clarification level must be met.

In the every day business people practice this types of reporting structures, which are analytical reporting, informational reporting and the proposal. We must know that a business report is an objective and orderly communication of facts and information that serves to the companies purpose (Lasikar, Flateley, and Rentz, 2008).

The analytical report focuses on examining problems or issues and advices immediate action. Analytical reports sometimes act as proposals, which define or identify the issue and looks for specific ways of solving the problem. Managers tend to use analytical reporting when one needs to identify an issue on a specific topic. This type of report breaks the problem into component parts to see how it is place together. The analytical reporting may be a memo or letter; it could have table of contents, glossary of terms, executive summary, recommendations, conclusion, it covers everything. The analytical reporting is very detailed and extensive.

While the analytical report is very detailed oriented the informational reporting is just about that, informing. When using informational reporting we present facts, we collect data and gather ideas on a specific subject. An informational reporting can be done in an informal way or a more formal way, that would have, table of contents, introduction, body, conclusion. It depends on the subject of which you are reporting and the seriousness of it.

The proposal focuses on an act of placing forward something for consideration. When a manager makes a business proposal, it should be organized, well written, clear, persuasive and effective. A proposal consists of characteristics like an executive summary, statement of need, research plan, problem statement, specific aims, plan of work, evaluation, and others (IUSB). The most important report of any business would be the proposal report. These three types of structures of reporting are different, however, they have similarities.

Every manager in a company must have basic management tools that he/she uses for decision making process. In small companies sometimes reports aren't needed as much as in larger companies where much more people are working and doing multiple activities. The two large groups reports are divided are informal and formal reports.

The informal reports focuses on getting information and organizing it. This type of reporting is informative and investigative. Even though the informal report isn't "formal" it does not mean it isn't important. In the informal report a manager would use the information report for the structure. This way a manager can record the day to day activities being held at a company, but also make monthly reports as well. It focuses on investigating, studying performance but not analyzing the information. When doing an informal report it should be kept simple; there should be any drawing of conclusions or giving recommendations. If informal reports are being written it should be clear, simple and effective (letter or memorandum), though most informal reports are usually in the form of person to person communication.

Formal reports are more serious than the informal ones. Usually managers use analytical reporting and proposal when making a formal report. When doing a formal report we should choose if its going to be a statutory report, which has to be prepared and presented in a procedure laid down by the law, or the non-statutory report, which doesn't required any type of law form.

On the basis of a frequent problem or issues there are two types of reporting. Routine or periodic report: consists of presenting reports on regular intervals. Reports may be submitted daily, weekly, monthly, annually, etc. Special reports: consists of reporting in a single occasion due to a special situation.

When the reports are based on the function, managers might use; informative reports, which as I already said presents facts of an issue or problem, or we can use the interpretative reports (also known as analytical), which consists of analyzing the facts, drawing conclusions and giving recommendations.

When dealing with problems that have been dealt with we can use technical reports, performance reports, problem determining reports and facts-finding reports.

It is imperative that a manager knows how to make a good report, some characteristics that are very important while doing a report are; precision: the report should be clear and to the point. By being precise it gives coherence to the report. Accuracy of facts: the reports should be made with honesty, everything said or written should be true and accurate. Relevant: the report should be made for a reason, when people do an irrelevant report it just confuses more the situation. Other characteristics would be brevity, clarity, objectivity of recommendations that would be made, simplicity (language wise), etc.

While preparing a report the person should take notes, investigate the source of information, analyze the data, make an outline and write the report, of course. When a person does a report, this one must be signed by the person submitting it and also dated.

The importance of giving a well written and very precise report is that it can be helpful to a persons career, as the report gives all the relevant information related to the topic, while poorly written reports may cause problems for a person because the credibility of his work gets on stake. In a certain way reports are a way of effective communication. In which we analyze a person's knowledge and skills.

CHAPTER XIV

Innovation

"Innovation is not the product of logical thought, although the result is tied to logical structure."—Albert Einstein

When we talk about the different aspects that a manager must have in order to be successful in his developing career we can mention some. They are actually in order, so the people begin to develop them one by one, in levels of importance and use them as the base for the others; the last one is innovation, but I actually think is one of the most important since nowadays the competition in the business world is turning more and more complicated and people is looking for new things; ideas that are INNOVATIVE, and those ideas are the ones who sell the more because people are used to the old things, and somehow they want new things that fulfill their needs in a different, even entertaining way and also make their lives somehow easier. In some cases, there is not the opportunity to create new ideas or products, but it could be to actually change something like the process of developing a process, or even the personal way of acting. Nevertheless, people must take care about those ideas, because they could think they are developing an innovative one and the final result could not be the expected one. That is why people need time to develop it, because it takes time of experience to learn how to develop and apply it.

Innovation is defined by Luecke and Katz, from the organizational point of view, as: "[Innovation] is generally understood as the successful introduction of a better thing or method. [It] is the embodiment, combination, or synthesis of knowledge in original, relevant, valued new products, processes, or services."

The actual word INNOVATION comes from the Latin word innovatio or innovare, which means to renew or change, so as we can see the actual term is indicating that it deals with a renewal of things that at a time takes you to a constant improvement in your professional or even personal life. People must learn to change the way they act, take decisions, do things; here is the perfect time to apply the advice that says that if we want different results, we must to the things in a different way as well. Joseph Schumpeter was a political scientist that applied the term "creative destruction" and said: "innovation changes the values onto which the system is based". That is why when you change the way of doing things, then the whole environment changes as well in order to improve that new aspect, and that is exactly when innovation happens. This is the reason why people describe innovation as something that must be done and performed and not something that just is.

People use to confuse the term innovation with invention; innovation is an idea that serves as a base for developing something new that will create improvement; basically innovation is the applied version of the original idea, and invention is the manifest of an idea. For example, in business, innovation is when the ideas turn into cash and invention is when you turn the cash into ideas; is the opposite.

The term innovation applies to all the different areas of life: business, sociology, technology, entrepreneurship, design and even personal life. By mentioning this, I would like to introduce an example dealing with the design area, more specialized in the fashion design. The fashion business environment is, nowadays, developing at a huge rate; is causing tremendous impact in society due to the incredible advance in the market and the influence it has on people. Due to this, there is a huge level of competition, and as in every single market everyone wants to be number one, the fashion industry is not getting out of this competition.

In the fashion industry, also known as the "creative industry", innovation is one of the most important aspects in order to be successful. For being successful here you must be passionate about what you are doing, then creativity and innovation are the bases of a successful career in the fashion world, and at present design and fashion industries go hand in hand with business and innovation.

Let's use the designing part of fashion. Designers have a big challenge, since they must constantly improve their collections because there is a lot of competition. They work with creativity, they innovate clothing with ideas that are based on cultural and social influences, and they design usually for each change of season or sometimes for particular events. The collections are created with the use of different types of fabrics, colors, and ideas that stick to the designer's vision. They are seeking for a particular aspect that differentiate them from the rest of the designers; something that makes them UNIQUE. John Galliano, designer of the house Christian Dior and Givenchy, refers to another designer's style (Stephen Jones), by saying: "What really makes Stephen's millinery so unique is his personality, his elegance and refinement. Everything he does look blown together"; and he also said: "One desire that is getting stronger than all other demands remains the desire to be unique". In the fashion industry, if you want to be unique, you gotta be innovative. "All creation is just recreation—a new way of seeing the same things and expressing them differently"—Yves Saint Laurent.

The Academy of Management Journal 39 said: "Innovation, like many business functions, is a management process that requires specific tools, rules, and discipline." To develop the innovation in a person, you need to follow like a series of steps that help people through the process. These steps are categorized in order from one to ten and are listed as this:

> Place to dream: the work environment must feel comfortable for the person. It must allow the person to develop innovative ideas, like a font of inspiration, with colors and objects that motivate the person to think, and employees must be allowed to decorate their work spaces the way they want to in order to feel comfortable with being there. For example, Google's offices are like a playground since they need their employees to be creative, so in that way they feel comfortable and it also contributes to turn the commonly boring work into something fun.
>
> Play: keep on trying whether the idea results or not; play and have fun with them so at a time those ideas will improve and make the final result something just awesome.

Innovators must experiment with their ideas, which is the first factor that contributes to the development of creativity and innovation.

1+1= 3: this means that usually the uncommon combinations of ideas could result into something really good. This is when a person is super curious and is constantly searching for learn new things and after discovering something interesting, they start looking for a way to apply it to get advantage of it.

Watch people around you: this deals with asking, watching and trying new things. You must not stay closed just doing one thing; you must look the environment around you, look what is going on. Look other people's interest because that might interest you as well and then you can learn things about it from them.

Connecting up: in the work environment there must exist partnership, because you can ask for help to the people you work with, they could actually increase your knowledge about some things; through collaboration with others can bring new ideas. You could meet very interesting people from who you might learn a lot.

Create a remarkable customer experience: make your customers feel valued. They must feel that you care about them by trying to guess what they really want and give it to them in an innovative way. Is like a blend of a research of how people live, how they experience their own lives, how they learn, how they feel; after that you must let them know how good your products, services or ideas are and try to surprise them.

True myths: "Stories persuade in a way that facts, reports and market trends seldom do, because stories make an emotional connection"-Tom Kelley. This is basically to tell people things about real and true facts about your products, service or ideas by using metaphors and made-up stories. This is to create a different culture in your company and create tighter bonds between employees and customers by using creativity.

Fly: You first have to let your customers know that you care about them if you want them to "love" you. You must apply a different vocabulary like using friends instead of customers, I mean treat them differently from other companies so that they would prefer to be with you, and that will create loyalty towards your company.

Do what you can do better: develop an idea and then REALLY apply it and make it turn into reality. Innovation will never exist if you just leave the ideas there; they have to turn into action, into something real. Here is where the managers apply the other aspects such as organization, planning, and some others to develop effective and efficient results.

Seek opportunities: once you develop innovation, then you are able to work with less resources because you will know how take the big part of everything and take advantage. Is to look for opportunities everywhere, so that you can work with everything and continue to do an innovative work. Innovation is basically the ability to see opportunities instead of threaths.

Now that we know the steps to take innovation into our lives, then we can mention some other important aspects about it. Innovation is commonly known as something that brings a lot of success to the companies because they are being renovated with something new and fresh; nevertheless, innovation has his consequences because as it benefits some companies it could also destroy others, why? Because some of them could not adapt to the new way of working or the ones that just stay the same always will be destroyed by those that are changing. So you must try to keep a balance between the old process and the new one so the company adapt step by step.

Innovators use tools as technology. Technology is their best resource and they implement it in the best possible way because it is part of their normal activities. Usually they become entrepreneurs due to the fact that they create new things, which are the principal aspect of an entrepreneur, and innovation is the difference between a leader and a follower because innovation sometimes means risk and leaders are the only ones who actually take risks because they are not afraid of failure.

In the template "Making innovation work: how to manage it, measure it and make profit from it", explains that innovation programs are usually based on 10 aspects which they listed like this:

Improved quality
Creation of new markets
Extension of the product range
Reduced labor costs
Improved production processes
Reduced materials
Reduced environmental damage
Replacement of products/services
Reduced energy consumption
Conformance to regulations

But if all of this works will depend on the ability of the company, whether if it manages well all of its resources in order to success. Sometimes the innovative ideas fail, and it is proved. Innovation is a very risky action for companies because as I mentioned before they could just not adapt to the new processes; that's why they have to measure each step in order to see if it is working in the expected way. If the failure is not well managed, then it will create a work environment full of tension and pressure that will affect every single part of the company. When innovation fails is because the ideas weren't accepted from all the personnel or they are just postponed for another time. For these reason failure must try to be detected before in order to omit all the consequences that it could bring.

So at the end we can easily see that innovation is very important in the people's lives because it helps them increase in every aspect, whether it is in business or personal life. It deals with changes, positive changes that will take them to improve and success. Nevertheless, innovation, if not measured, then can bring some problems since it is sometimes difficult to adapt to new situations, but changes are always good because that makes you unpredictable and it is known that people love new things, so they are attracted to innovative ideas and projects.

"Just as energy is the basis of life itself, and ideas the source of innovation, so is innovation the vital spark of all human change, improvement and progress"

XIV—A
Innovation and the Globalization

Mark Zuckerberg launched Facebook from his Harvard dormitory room on February 4, 2004. Today Facebook has over 600 million users and its revenue in 2010 surpassed 2 billion dollars. Zuckerberg is not only one of the youngest billionaires in the world—net worth: 13.5 billion being 26 years old—but also one of the leading personalities in the world, he was featured as the person of the year in 2010 and is currently on the forefront of technological innovation. I consider Zuckerberg to be a prime example of an innovative entrepreneur, which is a term that I use to refer to a person who transforms an idea into a successful business. Knowingly or unknowingly Zuckerberg built not only a fortune for himself but he changed the way communications, marketing, interactions, politics, society and business work—by innovating.

Innovating is basically doing something in a new or creative way. There are many contexts in which innovation can be used, but I will focus on innovation in a self improvement and business perspective. According to the Business dictionary innovation is the process by which an idea or invention is translated into a good or service for which people will pay, or something that results from this process.

Princeton press specifies two main types of innovation.

Product innovation: the introduction of a new product or a significant qualitative change in an existing product.

Process innovation: the introduction of a new process for making and delivering goods and services.

On a more personal basis innovation is defined as: rethinking the ways you do things on a daily basis and to improve with each passing day. It is important to have conviction in improvement in order to achieve innovation.

In business the crucial part of innovation is not to have an idea but to translate it into a good so it can be sold, this is where entrepreneurs strive and inventors perish. Entrepreneurs seek opportunities where others see problems. Innovative entrepreneurs know that having an idea is only the first step in the innovation process, after the idea is concretely formed it has to be transformed into something tangible—that is something that a leader does well, but the innovative entrepreneur is one that sells the tangible idea, generates profit from it, and experiences the ultimate freedom sought by all entrepreneurs. It is accurate to associate invention with innovation but invention is useful only to the inventor unless it is offered to the public, however niche that public may be. If the invention improves some product, process or service for the public, then that invention transforms into an innovation. This is what differentiates a mere invention from innovation; inventors create inventions, and entrepreneurs create innovation, what is the difference between these two? The entrepreneur manages to produce the invention and make it available to the public in a way that the public realizes that they need that invention.

The following questions have to be answered to successfully create innovation:

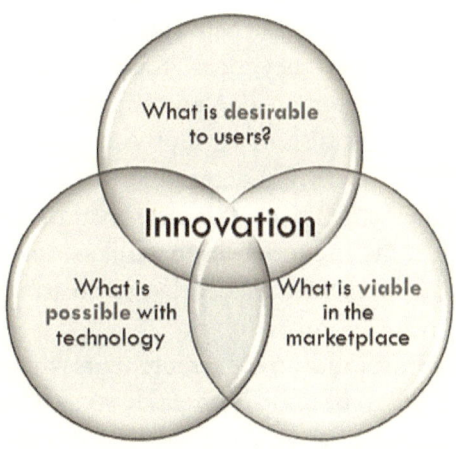

Link to this image is: http://www.ipprospective.com/burgeoning -business/innovation-as-an-investment-not-an-expense/

This image helps to illustrate how entrepreneurs view the process of transforming an invention into innovation. The new idea has to get a passing grade in each one of these three categories to give it innovation potential. An entrepreneur must have the observation skills and vision to answer these questions correctly and deliver a product that caters to a certain amount of population.

Great Innovators have been central in changing and improving different aspects of society. There are innovators in many fields, but some fields such as science, business, economics, medicine, and technology have the largest impact of society. To further understand innovation it is important to study some of its most important figures, and understand the impact that they have created in their specific areas. The capitalist economic system has given the opportunity to anyone to become a business innovator; this is evidenced in the United States more than in any other country in the world. As Fortune magazine puts It Practical Innovation—from the stream engine to the search engine—is the principal reason America achieved preeminence while other well-endowed land masses lagged or failed. Innovation is not simply invention, something to be measured by the number of patents or shrieks of "Eureka!" in the lonely lab. It is inventiveness put to use. As Thomas Edison admonished his associates, "We've got to come up with something. We can't be like those German professors who spend their whole lives studying the fuzz on a bee."

According to this same article great innovators have been characterized as obsessive, they press their ideas beyond its limits and have infinite perseverance. The author of the article claims that moneymaking was not a sustaining motivation for most of history's greatest innovators but rather a determination to bring a brainwave into the bustle of the marketplace. It is clear that great innovators think beyond personal fortune and recognition while selling their innovations to the public, most of them have a drive to create something bigger than life, and to create an impact on society.

I will mention some innovative entrepreneurs who put inventiveness into use and managed to become immensely successful in business and at the same time managed to enhance the lives of many.

Photography was invented in the 1830s but it became an established occupation by the 1870s. It required vast knowledge in chemistry, special equipment, and interest in difficult wet-plate processes. George Eastman in his early twenties worked with Rochester photographers George Monroe and George Selden, and developed a formula for gelatin-based paper film and a machine for coating dry plates. He started selling these plates in 1880. In 1885 Eastman patented the Eastman-Walker Roll Holder together with camera inventor William Hall Walker. Eastman's invention was a breakthrough because it allowed camera users to advance multiple exposures of paper fill through a camera. The roll holder that he invented defined the basic technology of cameras before the invention of digital photography. Eastman coined the term "Kodak" and started selling the personal camera for $25 and made photography available to a segment of wider range. Eastman kept expanding his business by buying patents and investing in research and development. In 1900 he introduced the "Brownie" camera which sold for $1 and for the first time made photography available for the masses; Kodak cameras were advertised as a necessity in every vacation. Making photography available for the masses gave Eastman an enormous fortune and placed him as one of the forerunners of innovation in America.

Some of the greatest innovators of the past decades are related to the dot com business; Pierre Omidyar is definably worth mentioning. He identified with the user-centered Apple rather than the business centered IBM, and started working for Apple writing graphics software. After several years of career he was already a millionaire but he is an idealist and wanted to use the internet as a platform to establish something greater. In 1995 Omidyar established the leading online auction site in the world: Ebay. The concept is very simple: Sellers could set their minimum prices, and buyers could then determine an item's market value by bidding up to what they'd willingly pay. A feedback system would allow users to rate each other, and in this way maintain a reliable online marketplace. He claims that with Ebay he wanted to give the individual power to be a producer as well. Today Ebay has become the biggest national marketplace in the USA. Omidayar based his idea on sheer simplicity, he didn't invent auctioning, he simply delivered it in a new format, and that is what has made him such a successful innovator.

"When most banks closed at 3pm, A. P Giannini kept his banks open until nine or ten at night for workers". Amadeo Peter Giannini has been called "America's banker." Son of Italian immigrants who established themselves in California in the 19th century; Giannini grew up in a time in which banks only gave loans and services to wealthy clients. The hard working immigrants were left outside. Giannini was angered by this situation and in 1904 he founded the Bank of Italy in San Francisco, this institution would cater to the banking needs of the masses. For the first time in America's history a bank that offered savings accounts and loans to the poor was opened. Skeptics were baffled when they came to know that that within the year the bank had deposits of over $700,000 dollars. After the earthquake that struck San Francisco in 1906 Giannini set up a temporary bank immediately, and made his reputation by helping the city rebuild. Afterward he expanded his bank across California, and broke the tradition of local banks that only favored wealthy and powerful customers. Giannini's bank focused on immigrants, and this was the factor that lead to its expansion—in the early 20th century immigrant communities were sprouting everywhere in America. In 1930 Giannini formed the Bank of America which would eventually become the largest in the United States. The bank become a symbol of the American economy, as it withstood the Great Depression, and funded the growing movie industry as well as the construction of the Golden Gate Bridge.

What do all these great innovators have in common? They had a drive, which was larger than creating a profit for themselves, they gave the market what it needed at the right time. They did not invent anything; they simply transformed older inventions by making them available to a large amount of people in a simple way that enhanced their lives. After reading about the lives of these great innovators the distinction between inventor and innovator becomes much clearer.

Innovation is a natural aspect of humanity; it will always occur as long as there humans on the planet. Without innovation, people and companies therein would be left trapped in the "comfort zone" which falters progress and development. Innovation is necessary to take a company out of the commodity trap. To better understand corporate innovation I will demonstrate examples of companies which have grown through innovation.

According to innovation zen Harley Davidson, Google, and Apple are all leaders of innovation. Harley managed to transform their image from motorcycle manufacturer to dream fulfiller. They accomplished this by focusing on the user experience rather to just selling products. They want their customers to be successful and realized as human beings. Apple also learned how to focus on user experience and achieve great success. Apple took advantage of the complexity of online music distribution and the out of date music reproduction systems to create the Ipod, a device that would become the worldwide symbol of music reproduction. Apple's customers are so loyal that they make up for most of the companies' marketing force. Another company that stands out is Google, not only has it become a household name ("google" it) but it has become the dominating search engine because It created superior user experience. Instead of having information organized into directories and folders the founders of Google, Sergey Brin and Larry Page decided to use an indexed search, which allowed users to find what they were looking for by a simple search query. Google has further innovated by complementing its search engine with applications such as Google Earth, Gmail, Google Reader and Google News, all of these make Google one of the leading internet portals in the world.

But what makes these companies successful innovators? According to Forbes magazine it is a set of innovation capabilities:

- At the ideation stage, an ability to gain insight into customer needs and an understanding of the potential relevance of emerging technologies.
- At the product development stage, an ability to engage actively with customers to prove the validity of concepts and to assess market potential and risks, and the ability to leverage existing product platforms into new products.
- At the commercialization stage, an ability to work with pilot users to roll out products carefully but quickly, and to coordinate across the entire organization for an effective launch.
- Some companies' strategy is to develop leading-edge products.

In a business everything has to be measured, an innovation process is of no use if it is not measured thoroughly to make sure what changes and improvements have to be made. After identifying innovation the next step for a smart entrepreneur is to measure innovation and make conclusions from the data. According to innovationmetrics. org measuring innovation is an important issue, as business growth and profitability depend of innovation. Many companies measure the wrong things, or in some instances don't measure innovation at all. This is a great mistake because it reduces the amount of growth that a company can have if it measured innovation. The Boston Consulting Group discovered that the most common metrics used to measure innovation in company were: total funds invested in growth projects, revenue from new offerings, allocation of investments across projects, projected versus actual performance, average development time per project, number of projects that meet planned targets, and percentage of ideas funded. It is interesting to note that these were the metrics used by top management; the research showed that employees mostly use revenue growth and customer satisfaction to measure innovation. A combination of these metrics must be used to insure that the companies' innovation process is measured correctly. For better results there should be a measurement team for every new innovative project that reports the measurements to top management, they in turn will take the decisions that will affect the future of the project.

After researching about innovation I realized that it is crucial in the development of corporate and personal success. Many of the greatest things in the world were born from a innovative idea which was later delivered to a great amount of people. Innovation is the latest step in the dependency to independency pyramid as is one which defines how a person will apply everything that was learned during the previous steps. One of the reasons of failure in personal innovation is lack of conviction in that idea. For innovation to occur the message must be clearly transmitted to the people that surround you and without true conviction this is nearly impossible. We should innovate in different aspects of our lives, and program ourselves to be innovators by default. This will help us achieve greater success in our careers and business activities. I know that I still have a long way to go to reach the top of the pyramid were I become a true innovator, but what I am looking forward to is that every step in the process will prepare me for the final task of becoming an innovative entrepreneur.

XIV—B
Innovation Marking a New Era: Lifestyle and Applications

We have been learning all along that the best attitude to achieve to start on a journey in a professional career and find success is that of an entrepreneur. One of the most important roles of an entrepreneur is illustrated by the concept of innovation. Also, the human being works eagerly to innovate with technology nowadays to make people's lives easier and more practical. For these two reasons, innovation comes out to be necessary in the modern world: we need to at least understand it to learn to live with it.

The word innovation means many things to different people depending on the needs they have. In business, the objective of innovating is finding the way to increase value, especially from the customer's point of view. An organization may be pursuing employees or processes that will lead them to be innovative to increase their profits, to take them out of a place in the market where they became stagnant, or just because they are in the top of everyone else and they are planning to stay there. Even if a company's business is selling standardized products, innovation will always be helpful to develop other important factors conforming to the operations strategy such as production processes, creating a system for outstanding delivery, or a creative layout that will reduce lead time.

The definition in a dictionary says that innovation is "the introduction of something new: a new idea, method, or device; novelty"[11]. We can look at innovation as the introduction of new things, but also as improvement or renewing of something that already existed. Innovation allows us to make use of inventions and discoveries in order to develop new concepts and apply to daily life. Who would have imagined back in the 1700s, by the time of the Industrial Revolution, that one day people would be able to communicate instantly in different geographical spaces? Or, who would have imagined by then that people were going to be able to travel to a different continent in just a matter of hours? This is all possible thanks to findings and advancements made

---

[11]   Merriam Webster online dictionary. http://www.merriam-webster.com/dictionary/innovation.

by pioneers from different branches of study, driven in great part by a sense of innovation.

An extraordinary manager, as we have learned, needs innovation in his or her list of qualities. This characteristic, along with several others will lead a professional to become an entrepreneur with a strong vision and a conviction that he will be successful. Innovation is so important because it is applied not only to technology and business, but also design, sociology, engineering, economics, and experimental sciences in general.

An early model of innovation called the "linear model of innovation" suggested that the correct sequence was going from Invention to Innovation to Diffusion, implying the most important thing to start with was researching and experimenting, to then innovate and make your invention or discovery known. The truth is that actually innovation is required in almost every field, and this basic model has changed and taken many forms according to the field it is applied into.

For entrepreneurs, the common goals that may want to be achieved by innovating are:

- Creating new markets
- Improving processes
- Reducing costs in labor, materials, and energy
- Improving quality
- Contributing in the nowadays "go green" trend, by reducing environmental damage

Organizations are desperate looking for people that see things differently and are creative, not only for business matters but also personally. An employee that is able to notice and analyze situations from different points of view is prone to finding several different alternatives or solutions, that will result in better functioning of processes and maybe even costs reduction. Being solution-oriented and being capable of seeing the big picture in creative ways can help generate profitable ideas and strive for a global economy.

I read several articles and blogs about how to become that innovative employee everyone is looking for, to learn about what smarter people thought about the topic. The truth is that I did not find one that applied fully to what I was looking for, but here I am compiling the qualities I consider more important and also the ones I noticed were mentioned frequently.

1. Be flexible. If you want to be an innovator, it means you are open to changes. Innovation is all about new ideas and methods, so it is vital to become someone that is always willing to understand these new concepts and work easily adapting to changes. By being flexible you will be free from patterns and able to recognize opportunities when they are presented.

2. Take risks. This goes linked with the first point. It is not enough to recognize opportunities when they show up; it is much more important to evaluate that opportunity and be willing to take the risk to start with your enterprise. Bill Gates stepped out of Harvard and created Windows. When this happened, he had a vision that every computer in a household will be running Windows after he was done. Nowadays, he is one of the richest people in the world thanks to his company.

3. Be ready to make mistakes and fail. If your are the innovator, you are the first one in the enterprise with the idea, so if there is no previous guide to tell you how to do things, you will be the one acting, listing, scratching and starting over to find the correct process. This is the reason why it is ok to have failures at a certain extent. A famous tale about Thomas Edison says he made 10,000 defective light bulbs before the one that finally worked. His apprentice asked him if he wasn't tired of trying and failing every time, to which his answer was, "of course not, now I know 10,000 ways of *not* making a light bulb". That is the best point of view an entrepreneur can adopt. This goes well attached to a quote from an Indian journalist named Bhupesh Bhandari that says, "Failure is an inalienable part of entrepreneurship. It is the bedrock on which success grows".

4. Always have a plan B . . . and if possible, plan C. By carrying on a project that is founded on a brand new idea, you are prone to failures. Given the fact that something may come out wrong in the original plan, there should always be alternatives to replace it and avoid losses (of time, materials, etc., depending on the project) by continuing where it was left off. Some people consider, however, that planning for alternatives is ironic

because the innovator must have the conviction that plan A is the best to go. Nevertheless, I support the idea that a backup plan will be useful enough.

5. Find direction. Without orientation you will get nowhere. Alice was asking directions in Wonderland and they asked her which her destination was. Her answer was that she had none, so they replied that "then, it doesn't matter which way you go". Alice in Wonderland may be a little sassy to use as an example but this makes a point. If you have no direction, you will wander around without getting anywhere. Maybe you will arrive to a destination but it will not be a 'destination' if you did not know that is where you wanted to get to. The best way to guide yourself to find the correct path is finding out what you are passionate about.

6. Try things yourself. It does not matter if someone else tried before, if you do, you might discover or see things other people were not able to. Watson and Crick spent hours sitting on lab making observations on something their professors thought of as a waste of time. Today, they are known for the discovery of the existence of DNA and its model.

7. It is important to have a strong leadership. Visionaries with good management skills are necessary to carry on with an enterprise. In a certain way, innovating is creating your own luck, and if you have any doubts, you can ask Steve Jobs, creator of Apple, Inc. Years ago he was kicked out from his own company and is now doing the same with his other creation, Pixar.

Once someone develops the attitude, he or she must develop a plan to create an innovative project; but to enter innovation, there are certain steps one must follow. From the researching I made, I particularly considered one[12] a very good sequence of steps to open to innovation, from which I annotate here the most important:

- Creating a work environment that will trigger innovative thinking. If the workplace is too fixed and does not allow some

---

[12]   http://createtomorrowtoday.com/downloads/Ten_Steps_to_ Innovation_article.pdf

space for employees to show off their creativity, then innovation would be stagnated. Getting ideas from employees, which are the ones doing the actual work, is valuable.

- Exploring and prototyping to get the best design or the best model is the way you can develop the best out of your product. The truth is that if you don't get to make the best version of your product, someone else who calls himself your competition will innovate by making a better version. The idea is to try as many times possible making the most improvements possible to your idea.

- Creating unusual combinations that spark innovative hybrids. Knowing how to get out of the patterns and break rules is part of the attitude of a true innovator. Mixing things that don't match can actually become a great idea or can you lead you to another better idea. You want create something new, so put things together that no one else has before. Not only parts of something, but also procedures, techniques, layouts, etc. Just try.

- Be a good observer. By learning from people and things around, start asking yourself why and how. Watch people and find out what they are interested in. Learn from you environment to determine how innovative a product you can make out of the interests from your environment.

- Build up connections. Partnerships in this case result much better than achievements. Look at it this way: if you are making up something with which you will innovate, there is a really high probability that you will fail the first times you try. Achievements then will not be reached at the beginning. Loyal partners will stick with you until you make it work and will keep confidentiality to prevent anyone other to steal your idea.

- Make sure you have an excellent customer service. Make the customers feel good with you to help your product start to get known around. Customer experiences will determine in a great extent how successful your product will be.

- Turn ideas into actions. You need to get the required groups of people to get your project starting to move. If you need a designer, get one; if you need to build something, make sure you have the right amount of labor force; if you need an engineer, make sure you have one . . . ideas do not innovate by themselves so you need the people to help you translate the ideas in the product itself, or the method, or the service.

One good example of people that have accepted innovation as a lead concept in their strategy and has successfully imposed it in their entire system is the young owners of Google, Inc. Google is no longer simply a search engine, it has many additional items incorporated to their website that have propelled them to the top of the business. Items like Google Maps and Google Adsense are the product of collaboration of their personnel. The company requests each employee to take about one third of their time just thinking about new ideas to be added to their scripts. They have modeled their installations in a fancy way, with several rooms to relax and play, slides to get from one floor to another, and comfortable meeting rooms. This way of working creates a good environment within the organization and the whole company's method is supported by innovation in terms of exploding creativity from every single unit available.

Someone with the attitude of an innovator does not want to follow anyone; innovators want to be one step ahead of everybody. It is all about building new things or building over the work of others and stepping forward with it. I liked Paul Boag's phrase that said that "at the heart of innovation there is a desire to challenge preconceptions"[13]. It means that an innovator must be willing to break the rules and change set structures for improvement. The human being is naturally afraid of change, and that is why sometimes applying these ideas may turn out to be difficult. The world has recognized that this is a mistake, and there are countries that are adding new plans in their educational schemes to build more entrepreneurs.

Innovation is a concept that has become so popular in our global economy that people look forward to make business with countries that have been able to adopt the term. The International Innovation Index,

---

[13] "How to become an Innovator", by Paul Boag posted on Web Strategy. Can be read at http://boagworld.com/business-strategy/how-to-become-an-innovator/

as they also called it, was produced by the Boston Consulting Group, the National Association of Manufacturers, and the Manufacturing Institute[14]. The research that determines the measurement is based on the business outcomes on innovation and also the government's support for innovation through public policy. So, investors now can check the levels of innovation per country with the Global Innovation Index to help them make decisions. According to the last index published[15], Singapore has the highest level of innovation in terms of government effectiveness, and Zimbabwe has the lowest level. For a curious fact, Panama is in the position 61 out of a 132 countries measured.

Even when innovation is all hype among professionals, there are some people who do not embrace it as such. I found myself reading a post in a blog written by a professor at some university. He said innovation goes in hand with marketing to create an image for the products. He remembers when he bought his first digital camera. Comparing it with the old one, it had less features but, oh, it's digital and I got to have it. With technology push, it is the market the one who determines if a given product you have is obsolete or not. Similarly, we see how the modern toys for kids are limiting their imagination more each time. The Wii, for example gives the kid a pre-made world from the mind of the creators of the games played. By the time our grandparents lived, it would not be rare that they were handed a box so they could turn it into whatever they wanted. If the box was an airplane they could jump into it and imagine they are flying, or if not, it would set horizontally so girls could pretend it was a stove.

Innovation comes right as long as you accept it. It is true that many things are left behind with new stuff coming out every day, but we leave stuff behind at the same rate we get new ones. New stuff replaces what was already there. The one thing to do is embrace it or at least learn to live with at least the innovative items or methods that define our society's lifestyles.

---

[14] Global Innovation Index official website: http://www.global innovationindex.org/gii/

[15] The last index was published in March, 2009. Table found at http://www.globalinnovationindex.org/gii/main/analysis/showdatatable.cfm?vno=1.2

I will like to end this paper with an interesting quote I found from Albert Einstein that says, "Innovation is not the product of logical thought, although the result is tied to logical structure". You can seem to be out of your mind when you start, but at the end it will all make sense when you get to success.

XIV—C
Innovation in Business Management

It has been said over and over that for a company to succeed in today's competitive market, the company or business have to focus and depend on the implementation and acquisition of great, relevant knowledge on which to base its decisions. That is why its important that good decision making be part of the everyday business. Since business managers are becoming more aware of this, they have been taking innovative approaches to business management by unity and consistency towards a purpose, along with a working environment where the company, as well as the employees can develop and excel.

I think that managers with more experience have come to realize how much they influence and impact their subordinates and that most problems in companies happened because of lack of communication, between managers and their employees. An incompetent manager is one that because of her/his actions can dissatisfied customers, cause poor production and decrease employers performance. While an effective manager is all about trying to avoid this circumstances by implementing new and innovative management strategies.

Its been said that an effective manager is an innovative leader. For me an effective manager should be a person who is inventive, has common sense, ingenious; a person who isn't afraid of embracing new concepts or picking up on old ones. A person who has these qualities stands out from the rest of the managers because of hers/his genuine goodwill, extraordinary creativity, confidence in employees and respect of course. Other managers think they know it all, and just talk instead of listening, they micromanage and at the end destroy the work balance, which becomes a problem to the company (Smith, 2003). This type of managers cannot be compared to effective and innovative managers, which are persons who bend over backwards to use the competencies of the employees and improve the company.

There are many guidelines, principles and skills necessary for a person to be an effective manager, all which lend themselves to the advancement of admirable leadership (Humphrey and Strokes, 2000). The most important of all is communication, its as important for a company as it is for humans to breath; without it a company couldn't work. Communication is the practice of imparting or giving one's thoughts and ideas to another person or group. It's the most relevant skill in any organization and it is a two-way street; that is why is has to be established before any other managerial action (American Heritage, 2000). The thing is the majority of the performance problems managers tend to experience cane be prevented or eliminated completely by just setting and communicating expectations appropriately. That's why communicating skills is the most basic prerequisite for any managers success. Another basis skill would be of directing personnel appropriately. Leaders must learn to not just only give tasks but also listen to their subordinates, that way mutual trust and respect exists in the work environment. This also ensures that no managerial actions constrain subordinates willingness to respond fast to their given tasks (Findley & Amsler, 2003).

Workplace morale is closely associated with subordinates responsiveness to managers directions, which is another important responsibility of the effective and innovative manager. Managers must make sure that their employees who they are accountable for maintain a spirited and most important positive approach to the day-to-day grind. Managers should also avoid certain mistakes like passing their stress and negativity to their employers (Gish, 2003).

As I mentioned previously, a person must have certain elements that will make him/her successful, this include, the ability to direct people, maintenance and appreciation of respect and high morale in the work environment, ability to communicate effectively and the prevention of common workplace conflicts or mistakes.

Communication lies at the core of effective managerial practices, but it isn't always fully practiced in terms of behavior. By communicating rules, expectations and regulations within your group of subordinates, employers will feel less frustrated, hence, they will be less likely to fail at their given task (Cunning, 2004).

Effective and innovative managers must learn to fully listen to their employees thoughts and ideas. Applying, as well, as improving listening skills gives managers some kind of "edge", because it helps them to fully understand what may or may not be working in the day-to-day operations. The simple act of listening helps managers make better decisions and also earn employees respect. Managers should value this skill and set aside time in some staff meetings for subordinates to speak their minds about ideas or concerns (Humphrey and Strokes, 2000).

Another important aspect of communication is setting expectations. Managers must understand that employers can't surpass or meet expectations if there aren't any settle for them. Managers should be setting expectations of performance levels to each employee, in terms of their tasks and the organizations objectives and goals. The tasks and goals must be clear to each employee, also terms of desired results must be given. The subordinate needs to know how much work he/she has to do and in what amount of time should it be done (Findley & Amsler, 2003). When a manager communicates his expectations fairly and clearly he/she is doing a favor to themselves, to the employees, and must of all to the organization, because this process makes the subordinate have a clearer idea of their tasks, which makes them do it faster.

Other aspect managers should employ or practice is delivering instructions effectively. The concept may sound basic but it is essential in ensuring subordinates trust towards the manager and their willingness to comply with the objective. A manager should not be patronizing, condescending or unnecessarily harsh to their employees, the opposite, a manager should see himself/herself as part of the group he is accounted for, and deliver tasks in a way that shows appreciation for the work each individual performs.

The last but very crucial element an effective manager must attain is persuasion. Persuasion is use by most innovative leaders. Persuasion is an art, a technique of inducing people, rather than forcing something upon them. An innovative manager induces its employees to comply with tasks. The aspect of persuasion has its core in the concept that people who know and respect their manager will be willing and eager to take instructions from him/her and perform them with positive outcomes. At the end its all about communication, and that entails fully listening, setting achievable expectations, delivering clear instructions and utilize persuasion when one fails.

For some managers the idea of directing or telling people what to do might be overwhelming, but it's a responsibility they must do (if they don't they can't be managers or leaders for that matter). Nowadays innovative leaders use four main steps to direct their employees. These are telling your employees what to do, not how to do it, maintaining a mistake-friendly environment, motivate your employees and welcome outspokenness.

By telling the employees what to do, and not teach them how to do it you are given them trust. Most managers like to explain exactly how they want the subordinate to accomplish the work given, because they feel something is going to go wrong. This is something effective and innovative managers must learn to deal with. If a manager is always looking over the shoulder at its employees, he is doing a terrible job. First of all a manager should train their subordinates to the extent in which they could be trusted to do their tasks without someone breathing down their neck; and second of all a manager should have faith in his/her team. An innovative manager should even trust his/her subordinates to make decisions when he/she is not around. A manager should make sure that the team his/her is accountable for has all the information, tools and training needed to conduct a given task, so he/she can then step back and let the others do their work. This conduct should be essential in today's work environment because of the everyday events that take place so rapidly and unnoticed. The managers should restrain themselves and just give subordinates their task and then leave the subordinate so he/she can fulfill the task he/she is clearly appropriate to do. This way hesitancy and tension is cut off from the workplace and helped employees to not only feel trusted but fulfilled, because they know their actions will be appreciated rather than picked apart by a micromanager (Freedman, 2000).

An effective and innovative manager must maintain a mistake-friendly atmosphere, so he/she can accomplish the freeing of employees. It is better for everyone in the work environment, if subordinates are accomplishing their tasks without someone guiding them through every step of the way. If a subordinate fails in their task, he/she can learn from its mistake so it wouldn't happen again. When an employee makes a mistake he has to go back and trace what went wrong, and by seeing that a decision was ineffective or inadequate she/he wont make the same mistake again. It is better this way, to see clearly the mistake, instead of having a manager yelling at you. An innovative manager always expects success from their employees but if there is a situation where the subordinate has made an honest mistake; the manager must know that the best policy is to value the experience of the mistake for its learning potential and then move on. There is not reason to dwell on past mistakes that won't be able to mend.

There are some cases were even thought managers give their employees all the information, planning, training and resources, employees are still unmotivated and indifferent about their work and tasks. That's when managers have to turn to motivation. They have the responsibility of encouraging their subordinates so that they can give their best to the organization. First of all managers must ensure that employees on lower levels feel like their doing something meaningful to the driving factors of the company. One way of doing this is making high-lever employees mingle with lower level ones. This solution might be effective and will help lower level employees have a more clear vision of the goals and objectives of the company. Managers should be thankful of every subordinate even the one with the most insignificant job, that way they feel like their effort is noticed and they will be working with in a more positive and enthusiastic way. By challenging them, they developed and do their job more effectively. One sharp and dedicated employee is more worthy than 4 or 5 who are unmotivated and uninterested in their tasks.

When directing people is good to invite outspokenness. This means to welcome people to talk and speak up their minds with no judgments. By welcoming outspokenness managers are giving a direct acceptance to subordinated input (Freedman, 2000). Employees should not be expected to remain quiet, when they feel they have a better idea or solution for something. A subordinate whose ideas are ignored and put off, usually start feeling unmotivated and neglected from the organization, so managers should be very careful with this matter. An effective and innovative manager should treat their employees as an indispensable member of their team, not just as another worker; and an employee shouldn't be invited but expected to share his/her thoughts and ideas. An innovative leader will put in action all of these elements previously stated so the company can flourish. All of this things that are done for the employees, in the long run bring lots of benefits to the organization.

Any business no matter what their product is or what their doing, cannot work with excellence if there isn't a high level of respect, as well as morale. An innovative leader knows that this element is imperative for boosting enthusiasm for any kind of job or tasks. Several ways this high respect and morale can be achieved is by hiring carefully. Managers must be careful with the people they hire (Gish, 2003). An employee who has inconspicuous qualities should not be hired. Managers should ignore the shortage of morale when hiring subordinates. Its true every single human being have undesirable qualities, that's what makes us humans. But an employee who is consistency lazy in the work environment, selfish or incompetent in his/her task should not be considered for employment. An effective and innovative manager is very judicious when hiring, managers like to have the best they can work with them.

Once a manager has a great team of subordinated its only fair that he/she celebrates the accomplishments of the employees. A manager should make the subordinates stay interested and challenged. A good idea is to establish a recognition program that rewards the employees, not only acknowledging their work. Rewards doesn't have to be always monetary (thought it's the way everyone would like to be rewarded), it can be a lunch, a gift, something that is sincere. Some may say that why should employees be rewarded, if they are already rewarded with a paycheck? By being an innovative boss you have to consistently show your appreciation for the employees hard work. Individual incentives, as well as group recognitions programs are all great ways of boosting the employees spirits (Gish, 2003).

Another way to maintain the respect and morale of your subordinates towards you is to stand behind your people, have their back. By providing support they feel more confidence of themselves. Effective managers must stand behind their subordinates when their doing things right and when they make mistakes. By having their back employees respect and trust you more in your decision-making.

An element that helps boost subordinates confidence and respect towards you is to be available. People don't like working for someone who is never around. As a manager, you must make yourself available to your employees. Innovative leaders, as well as managers throughout the years have put in practice the "open-door" policy, which encourages the employees to come to you, if they have any doubt or any questions about their tasks. Managers must make employees feel welcome to ask anything and to have no fear. If employees feel like their going to be yelled at they are not going to come to you, and they may make a mistake, because they had fear of asking you something (Giuliani, 2002). Also managers must make sure that employees know where is your office or if you are not there, who is in charge.

I think managers should apply all of these elements. It will definitely help them have a more positive effect on the office. Managers shouldn't lose focus of their morale and their employees morale.

Sometimes despite all of the aspects and elements given for innovative and effective managers there are things that cant be controlled, and something eventually will go wrong whether is a big problem or an insignificant one.

Innovative managers should know that they don't have to know it or do it all. They have employees who were hired in the first place to help them, so managers should use employees abilities. Every employee comes with different qualities and abilities. So its important for a manager to know the subordinates abilities and so he/she can employ them into their tasks. Some managers tend to focus on subordinates weaknesses instead of their strengths (Cunning, 2004). Managers who do this are losing time and focus. Even thought managers should also mentor, coach and guide subordinates so that they can overcome their weaknesses, its not a bad thing to tailor their tasks according to their individual abilities. An effective manager never focuses on the employers weakness, but the opposite, makes use of his/her talents.

An effective and innovative manager is always there for his/her employees. Managers should maintain a good attitude. Bad managers usually tell their subordinates they are too busy to help them or they are too critical. Managers must listen to their team. Managers should treat their subordinates with the same respect, you want from them.

Also by praising accomplishments, achievements and dedications employees feel more confident. Managers should praise liberally to everyone who has done a good work. Even day-to-day actions are sometimes worth praising (Cunning, 2004).

The innovative leader avoids mistakes in the work environment by following the rules previously mentioned, use subordinates abilities, be personable and welcoming, and praise liberally. When a manager follow these rules he/she creates an avoidable pitfalls workplace, in which people are always positive and enthusiastic.

For an average person to become an effective manager and an innovative leader he/she should follow the principles, elements, aspects and rules already stated. They aren't very time-consuming but they are habits that with time will be easier to employ and wont be something that you should be reminded of, but it would come off naturally. If a person takes the time to become innovative with himself/herself, as well as its work place, their employees, as well as his/her family would be happier and more productive.

XV—D
How to be an innovator

WHAT IS INNOVATION?

An idea or invention (created by knowledge, experience, imagination, a 'lucky accident' or any combination of these) Developed into something new or improved that generates wealth and/or social good.

My initial perception of an innovator was merely someone that creates a product or a service that simply replaces another, giving better prices or services. After reading up on the subject in different websites on the Internet and also reading a book called book "Start-up Nation" I realized that Innovation is not just about having an idea, having the passion, or being able to fill a need. It is a collection of these three things, that's what makes a true innovation, having an idea that fills a need that you're passionate about. Like many things in the business world to be an Innovator there are certain steps one must follow, I came across many web sites showing quick and easy steps for becoming an innovator like: "*Choose area for innovation, Gather knowledge Break problem into pieces, Fit in gaps with solutions*" and "*hour of quiet time, Seek inspiration, jot down whatever comes to you, Take immediate action*". To me the only thing these websites give you is the basic and most simplest idea anyone would have for the question *what is an innovator?*, coach Marv Levy, head coach for the 90's buffalo bills, used to say "football is simple you just have to: run, pass, catch, tackle, and kick better than the other team". With this explanation anyone who has never heard of the sport would actually think its pretty simple.

"Start-up Nation" is book about all the innovations that Israeli inventors and entrepreneurs have brought to its country and the world, it states that excluding the United States Israel has the most companies listed in the NASDAQ than any other country. There are some cases and examples that I will be citing in this research paper from the book, I got interested in this it apart from the obvious reason that I'm Jewish, because Israel is or maybe I should say was a country with lot of needs, some more simple than others, but all important like the need to defends itself or the need for water in the Negev (southern desert). Israel was built on the shoulders of innovators like Simcha Blass(right side) who invented the drip irrigation system and planned the first water pipeline to the Negev before Israel's creation, and Major Uziel Gal(left side) who invented the UZI sub-machine gun which provided Israel with an effective, simple and inexpensive Firearm for its many wars to come.

Find a Need That Intersects With Your Passion

Passion: Capable of, having, or dominated by powerful emotions. I prefer the definition I got from my brother "the one thing that you would do at 5 am on a Sunday morning". In my case I wouldn't accept a job that would require me to wake up at 5 am, unless that job would be professional football player, which I would gladly wake up at 4 am.

Sometimes the need and the passion could be that of your homeland as in the case with General Israel Tal, an armored-division commander in Sinai Peninsula during the Six-Day War, Israel Tal(below Right) was the creator of the Israeli armor doctrine which led to the Israeli successes in the Sinai in the Six Day War. He also led a development team to create the first Israeli main battle tank *The Merkava Mark* I (below left), which took into consideration Israel's battlefield characteristics and lessons learned from previous wars, which were that Israel couldn't win a war by attrition, crew survival and rapid repair are prioritize, In 1970 Israel decided it needed an independent tank-building capability due to uncertainty of overseas sales for political reasons.

Israel Tal had a passion, sort of (survival of his men) and he had a need (Israel's need for armament). So he began the development and building of Israel's Merkava tank, it is designed for survivability and for rapid repair of battle damage; it has a rear entrance to the main crew compartment allowing easy access even under enemy fire. This allows the tank to be used as a platform for medical disembarkation, a forward command and control station, and an armored personnel carrier.

Tal organized the armor into the leading element of the Israeli Defense Forces, characterized by high mobility and relentless assault. Starting in 1964, General Tal took over the Israeli armor corps and re-trained all Israeli gunners to hit targets beyond 1.5 km. In open terrain, such long distance gunnery proved vital to survival of Israeli armor corps for subsequent wars. Its mobility is considered comparable to the German Blitzkrieg and many hold it to be an innovation of that tactic.

We can see clearly how passion in something greatly raises your efforts towards it and the need for it increases the marketability, Israel Tal was one of the many innovators we can pull that example from but to me he seemed the most interesting.

Be Assertive, Persistent, and Question Everything

Start-Up Nation, practically the book on Israeli innovation, talks extensively about this, the persistency of the Israeli when questioning his superiors and just their whole attitude of doing things is called *chutzpah*, which can be roughly translated to sheer guts, this behavior can be seen everywhere in Israel: the way students speak with their professor, employees challenge their bosses, and sergeants question their generals. This behavior is nothing new, throughout biblical history we see many books coming together from debates and arguments between rabies, like the Talmud and the Guemara.

> "Israelis are thought from age Zero to challenge the obvious, ask questions, debate the obvious . . . Innovate"
> -Shmuel Eden

An Example of Questioning the norm is a story told by Shmuel Eden, leader of Intel Israel operations. Throughout history of modern computers processing speed determined how fast was your computer, this became the law for chips (fast clock speed small size) that IBM, Wall Street, and the business press followed. Business was booming until the 2000's "The Power Wall". More power meant more heat for the chips, the solution was simple insert a fan to cool them down, but there wasn't a fan small enough that could be inserted into laptops, the Israelis predicted this and offered solutions that didn't follow the same doctrine (fast clock speed small size) and pitched it to headquarters, but got shot down because of the same.

The Israeli team didn't give up on their idea of splitting the computer chip's workload; they spent almost a week every month in Santa Clara, California were Intel's headquarters were located trying to convince the board that they were right and the world was wrong.

It took them 3 years but they finally convinced CEO Paul Otellini to approve their chip, which later took the name of *Intel Centrino.*

The switch to the Israelis team approach came to be known as the right turn within Intel, because of this sales grew by 13% from 2003 to 2005. By 2006 profits plunged 42% luckily the Israeli team stepped in once again to save the day with they're latest innovation, dual-core processing which came to be known as Intel Core 2 Duo.

Israel's Intel team questioned almost 20 years of production and company tradition; they were persistent to make their idea into reality, and they were assertive in their research and meetings with they're superiors, because of this they revolutionized the computer chip industry. What we can take from this story is basically to question, debate, and challenge anything and everything around your idea, even if it has been in place for 20 years it can still be wrong or it can be improved in some way, you can never be scared to tell someone that they're wrong if you know that you are right even if it your direct superior.

"Go far, Stay Long, See Deep, Work Hard"

Long before there was a state of Israel there were already boycotts from the Arab nations that could be traced back 100 years. In the midst of this Israel embraced the Internet, software, computer, and telecommunications. Orna Berry, an Israeli venture capitalist mentioned, "High-tech telecommunications became a national sport to help us fend against the claustrophobia that is life in a small country surrounded by enemies". It is estimated that the total costs of the boycotts against Israel has a range between the 100 billions, but the opposite is just as valuable, the attributes the Israelis have developed from the constant efforts of the Arab world to crush their country.

Gil Kerbs, a former member of the 8200(unit in the IDF specialized in cyber terrorism) just packed up and left for Beijing to study Chinese intensively, working with a private instructor for five hours a day for a full year, while also holing a job at a Chinese company, so he could build a business network there. Today one of his Israelis companies is providing China's largest retail bank with voice biometric technology.

Israelis are far ahead of their global competitors in penetrating such markets in part because they had to leapfrog the Middle East to find new opportunities, by the time Israelis are in there 20's they are tested in discovering exotic opportunities abroad, they are also unafraid to enter unfamiliar environments and engage cultures very different from they're own.

One example of this Israeli internationalism is Netafim, and Israeli company that had become the largest provider of drip irrigation. Netafim was created by Simcha Blass, born in Warsaw, Poland, to a Jewish orthodox family. He was active in the Jewish self-defense units organized in Warsaw to defend Jews during the end of World War I. His engineering studies in Warsaw were interrupted by the Polish-Soviet War and completed after that war. During the war, he was recruited to the Polish Army, there he invented for the Polish Air Force, a meteorological appliance, measuring the intensity and direction of winds.

In the early 1930s, Simcha drew his attention to a big tree, growing in his backyard "without water". After digging below the apparently dry surface, He discovered why: water from a leaking coupling was causing a small wet area on the surface, This sight of tiny drops penetrating the soil causing the growth of a giant tree provided the catalyst for Blass's invention.The drip irrigation concept was born and experiments that followed led Blass to create an irrigation device that used friction and water pressure loss to leak drops of water at regular intervals.

In the late 1950s, with the advent of modern plastics during and after World War II, he took a major step towards implementing his idea. After leaving government service in 1956 he reopened his private Engineering office and worked with his son Yeshayahu on the drip irrigation idea. The main aspect of the new invention was to release water through larger and longer passageways Larger passageways prevented the blocking of tiny holes by small particles. In the early 1960s, Blass developed and patented this method and the new dripper was the first practical surface drip irrigation emitter.

Netafim was pioneering the industry because it developed an innovative way to increase crop yields by 50% while using 40% less water, Netafim was having no hesitation about traveling in pursuit of desperate markets in need of its product, As a result it operates now in 110 countries over five continents it has offices from Japan to Peru. Netafims product became so indispensable for countries that are mostly desert like the 22 Arab states surrounding Israel that thy opened diplomatic channels between most of them.

"Go far, Stay Long, See Deep" this is a quote from Outside magazine, what I wanted to portray with it was the fearlessness of the Israelis to go to a place they haven't been before and start a life there, the clearest example of this is my boss Kfir Avital, he was an air force engineer but here he is in Panama and now holds a very high position in the chain retail stores of El Titan. To be an innovator you cant be afraid to change your setting and travel in search of new opportunities that could be discovered anywhere even here in panama.

To sum it all up to be an innovator you have to be feerless: to seek new opportunities, to be passionate about something, or to challenge your own existence. You mustn't let anyone bring you down.

"I have not failed. I've just found 10, 000 ways that won't work."—Thomas Edison

There are many ways to define innovation. Some people state that innovation is equal to invention, which I believe is wrong. The main difference is that innovation is about discovering new ways of doing something that was done before. Others believe that innovation is about improving existent things, processes or products. In this paper I want to offer actual social problems we are facing and studies made by prestigious universities. Moreover, I as a future executive want to provide solutions for current social and business problems by putting innovation into function.

I believe that our world is in need of people who can see a little further, people who can find efficient and effective solution to problems such as education, public health, social mobility and poverty, for instance.

Innovation can not be reach from night to day. It is a long and complex way. Today we are seeing how some billionaire people did even finish college, for example, Mark Zuckerberg the creator of facebook and Bill Gates an entrepreneur that found Microsoft.

However, not going to the university does not mean they did not prepare themselves since they were children to be in the position they are right now. Facebook, without any doubt, has been one of the greatest innovations in the communication ground. Before facebook was My Space which is also a social network, but facebook surpassed it by innovating and including videos, albums and advertising within user's profiles. If it is analyzed with details Facebook was not the first on the market but certainly it was the one who innovate the most among all the competitors. Google and Yahoo is another good example. Prior to Google was Yahoo which used to controlled the market. Yahoo had a large and complex menu before Google appears; the latter took advantage of this and create a friendlier and more efficient menu that as we know surpassed Yahoo. As I mentioned before, Bill Gates is a clear example of innovation. He improved something that already exist and at the same time created new products from that. As it can be seen with these examples, being the first is important but does not mean the most successful ones. All these companies are constantly competing and the advantage of one to another is how innovative they can be.

According to the Cambridge dictionary an entrepreneur is "someone who starts their own business, especially when this involves seeing a new opportunity." Innovation is something that can be learnt or to prepare for. There are different ways to prepare myself as a manager to become an entrepreneur, the one that I consider the most important is by applying innovation into my daily life since a child. For example, right after I receive my monthly payments from my parents I could either spend it on regular things or in other things that will produce a bit more money. Other example could be, making an excel sheet to display everything about my consumption so I can realize where I am spending more and how to decrease that. By doing this little by little I would be able to implement those details into business in an easier and more efficient approach. Another way is by going to college and complementing it with work to be able to put into practice the theory learnt at universities. College will not give or does not mean success, but I believe is necessary to prepare yourself in some fields. Today, whether it is like it or not college is necessary to at least start working. Yet, the truth is that college will not teach you how to innovate, in fact, most of the business schools in Latin America and not very long ago in the US, entrepreneurship was not even on the subjects a student needs to graduate. I agree that universities in Latin America must include entrepreneurship on their subjects not just to meet professional requirements but to meet social requirements also. I as an active member of the society and future manager would like to be useful not just for companies but society and its needs. Innovation is needed in many fields and I believe is the smartest way that a government has to face economic, social and educational problems.

It does not matter which countries are visited in south, central or North America the educational system does not work in any of these. In any of these regions the students are taught to be innovative, there is an old and obsolete method of teaching. A study made by the Inter-American Development Bank (IDB) has revealed that only one in three Latin American young people manage to obtain a secondary school education, while in Southeast Asia the number is 80 percent. Only half of primary school graduates in Latin America go on to finish their studies, compared to the 95 percent in Malaysia and Korea. I know that poverty and school desertion play an important role on this but in part is because of the lack of innovation. Today, there is almost any product that has not been manufactured in some Asian country and almost all the technological innovation is from there. Maybe that is why some countries in Asia are taking over of the world economy, leading and improving it. Asian countries have changed their educational system at the same time world changes.

The educational system has not changed in many years, and the world has certainly done it. The way businesses are done today differ very much from those that were done 20 yeas ago.

Most of the time, public schools complain that the budget for them is too low to offer good educational quality. There are many ways to innovate in the educational field and deal with the budget problem. First, a way I found interesting is by offering art and sports courses to prepare students to be very good at these.

Second, after learning one of these courses properly, the student can be eligible to do an internship on a company on that specific field and continue learning. Both the student and the company will benefit. The student will have a workplace and will be able to continue learning in real life. Also, the student can be able to compete in equal conditions with those that are graduated from private schools. On the other hand, companies will have qualified people working for them "at no cost". I say no cost because there will be a trial period to ensure that students are actually qualified but after period companies are required to pay the students.

Recently, Harvard University did a research about innovation. According to the study, innovators need to have "Discovery skills" that will distinguish creative executives. These skills are: associating, questioning, observing, experimenting, and networking. I personally believe that these skills are crucial but I will add some more because according to what I have learnt and read there are a series of steps in order to achieve innovation. An innovator must have an extraordinary common sense that allows him or her to differentiate good from excellent decisions. Innovation needs a lot of judgment because the individual will have many options and needs reasoning and critical thinking at the decision making process. Now, coming back to the skills described by Harvard University, associating, I believe is one of the most important. At the moment to innovate is crucial to associate the needs and opportunities of the product or service that I am working on. In addition, associating is about relating ideas with questions, information and opportunities.

If I as a manager start innovating in something that will barely growth my company then all the effort and money needed to innovate on something will be wasted.

Innovate is very expensive and take quite a long time for that reason observing and analyzing the market is vital in order to obtain results.

As every business plan, innovation process needs an experimenting stage or period. Before going into a major investment I as a manager would like to prove the effectiveness of the product in a minor scale. This will help me to predict the behavior of the market and to forecast results.

Example: Valeria Valderama, I am a Venezuelan living in Panama, and I have seen how Venezuelan people have come to Panama to try to "innovate" and they have failed. Consequently, most of them have lost a lot of money here in Panama. I believe one of the major causes is because they believe that just because their products works in Venezuela, it will also work in Panama, that idea is completely wrong. First, the markets in both countries are completely different. Venezuela has a population of over 30 millions people and its economy relies on oil production and natural resources mostly. On the other hand, there is Panama which population is almost 3 million people and its economy relies on the Panama Canal and the free zone in Colon. The culture is different even tough both countries are very near. Possibly what is normal in Venezuela it is not in Panama. For example, air conditioner business should be much more profitable in Panama because of the weather than in Venezuela. These are some facts that need to be taken into account before going into a major investment. To be innovative does not mean being successful, there is a process and key steps that need to be done before.

I have always heard that innovation is about future or the next step therefore to forecast what is going to happen next year is essential for entrepreneurs at the moment to innovate. I believe that to be able to forecast the market is necessary to have a clear view of the market and its behavior. Also, by studying the history because it is said that is cyclical.

Most of the greatest innovative products or services come from individuals who question themselves about them, for example, according to the Harvard research; Michael Dell famously created Dell Company with the question: "Why do computers cost five times the cost of the sum of their parts?." It seems like by question the Status Quo, I as a manager can be much more successful when innovating. Coming back to the Venezuelan's example, we should ask ourselves, what is really necessary in Panama? Are there enough parking lots on the city? In what I do, have the existing companies met the necessities of the market? Because if they haven't I can innovate and offer to the market what they really need. A way I found interesting is by being a one day customer and ask myself, what do I need the most? What would I do different than them? I believe the objective is to obtain the best field in which to innovate.

I as an innovator need to prioritize and do tasks in which I am really good at; if I am not that good I need to outsource them. I said this because when innovating I need to do the work in which I am the best at. To obtain data, knowledge and information and I require doing networking. Normally, I would think that the lesser people know about my plans, the higher the probabilities to be the first, but after reading and talking to other executives I have realized that everyone needs help and supervision. Moreover, specialist suggests that the individual needs to be the opposite of secretive, in fact, they ask you to show your ideas as many smart people as possible. I agree with this because two brains think more than one. It is impossible for me to have all the answer for all the problems I will face trough the process of innovation.

I consider that every innovation leader needs to have a mix of emotions and realism. It is impossible to innovate without feeling emotions; at the end it is being creating something "new". Yet, these emotions have to be combined with realism. The idea needs to make sense in all aspects, profitability, cost, implementation and length of it.

One of the most critical point I found at the moment to innovate is the ability to take risks. As every beginning, there is always an important percentage of failing, at the end until the product or service is out the innovator will not know for sure how the consumer will behave. I believe that in almost every innovative process there is a certain grade of uncertainty and a real innovator must know how to manage it.

Business and technology leaders are increasingly aware of the need to hit all possible sources of technologies and ideas, both internally and externally. But in many traditional, mature industries, companies still rely on their internal resources for the size of their development activities. A manager needs to know when and where to look for alternatives in case internal resources are not enough. Also, small companies that manage a much lower budget in research than bigger companies should be look externally to be responsive in what others are doing.

I think that there is a moment in which an entrepreneur must know whether the project will work or not. Innovation leaders have responsibility for the effective use of their company's resources. It is vital for an entrepreneur to have **the courage to stop projects, not just start them**.

As I mentioned before innovation is a process and entrepreneurs can not have all answers to problems. Innovation leaders play a critical role in assembling teams. Innovation is definitely a team effort, and that's why they focus considerable time and attention on this area. As every process there are some stages that an entrepreneurship will not be prepare for, that's why having a prepared and professional team will allow to obtain faster, effective and efficient results. I am sure that if we study every single case, Bill Gates, Mark Zuckerberg, and any other person that has innovate and being successful, we will see that their staff is so well prepared to be able to face all the challenges of innovation.

Procter and Gamble, IBM, HP, and other multinational companies spend millions in studies and staffing. At the moment of hiring the individual needs to meet all kind of requirements, not just knowledge but psychological as well. They make he applicant go through a very complex process just to know whether he or she is prepared for the job or not.

An entrepreneur must motivate all his or her staff. I think that if the staff is motivating enough the result of projects will be considerably higher from those that are not. Employees in most organizations would like to feel that their ideas make a difference in their workplace. For many people, in fact, there are few things more motivating than seeing or assisting the successful implementation of an idea they suggested. Some times managers think that should be them who create or innovate, not employees. This idea is clearly wrong, in fact, most of the innovative ideas can be created by employees rather than higher executives. What I would do is to challenge rather than extinguish them. I would ask my employees not to just identify problems but to bring solutions. Also, I would ask them to give me recommendations after they take a hard look to the complete process. It is not just to ask them for suggestions, is to put them into practice when necessary. A crucial part of this whole equation is the actual implementation of the great ideas generated by employees. Without follow up, the organization simply ends up with a long list of unused suggestions and a lot of frustrated employees. Managers should put the person who suggested a great idea in charge of the actual implementation. The initiator usually has that sense of ownership and is highly motivated to see his suggestion put into practice.

To sum it up, I think that it is time for human being to stop thinking just about being professional successful lone. It is not that difficult to complement and to be part of solutions to society's problems. I can not understand why there is such a poverty and educational problems in countries like Venezuela and Panama that manage great amount of money. It has been proved or demonstrated that innovation is a strong way to obtain professional and personal success. There is a huge market in social problems; I believe we just need people who combined personal with professional success.

CONCLUSION

Extraordinary managers make the whole greater than the sum of its parts. They add value to their organization. They get extraordinary results from ordinary people. Average managers wind up with ordinary results no matter how good their people are. There are even managers who, unfortunately, drag their groups down so that they get ordinary results from extraordinary people. The whole, then, becomes less than the sum of its parts. These managers have little, if any, value. They don't really manage much of anything. The steps presented to you are the foundation principles for development and unity across the organization. You and the organization becomes one and the legacy continues.

BIBLIOGRAPHY

http://www.imf.org/external/np/exr/ib/2008/053008.htm
http://en.wikipedia.org/wiki/Globalization
http://en.wikipedia.org/wiki/International_criminal_court
http://en.wikipedia.org/wiki/International_Court_of_Justice
http://en.wikipedia.org/wiki/Global_administrative_law
http://en.wikipedia.org/wiki/WTO
http://www.imf.org/external/np/exr/ib/2008/053008.htm

⇒ "Books—7 Habits of Highly Effective People—Habit 1: Be Proactive." *Dr. Stephen R. Covey.* Web. 02 May 2011. <https://www.stephencovey.com/7habits/7habits-habit1.php>.

⇒ "Non-Confrontational Tendencies in the Workplace." *CrossRoads Counseling and Career Consultation Center—Guiding Your Path to Wholeness.* Web. 02 May 2011. <http://crossroadsindy.com/counseling-and-mental-health-articles/non-confrontational-tendencies-in-the-workplace>.

⇒ Aguirre, Antonio. "El Sentido Común en los Negocios". Web article in internet blog spot:
<<http://aguirresoluciones.blogspot.com>>August 16, 2007.

⇒ Carson, James. "The 3 R's of Business Ethics". Web article, unknown date.
<<http://commonsenseteaching.com/the-3-r's"-of-business-ethics>>

⇒ García, Charles Patrick. "Un mensaje de García: sí, puedes triunfar" El Pricionero de Guerra conoce la batalla, page 95. Spanish Edition. Printed in Mexico, de Bosillo, 2006.

⇒ Gladwell, Malcom—Blink: The Power of Thinking without Thinking—El Lado Oscuro de la Seleción de Datos Significativos, Page: 90. Spanish edition: "Inteligencia Intuitiva". Published in January 11, 2005.

⇒ Goleman, Daniel. Emotional Intelligence: Why can it matter more than IQ? Spanish edition "Inteligencia Emocional en las Empresas". Printed in México in 1996.

⇒ Goleman, Daniel. Working with Emotional Intelligence. Spanish Edition: "La Inteligencia Emocional aplicada", page 159. New York: Bantam Books, 1998.

⇒ Griffin, Ricky W. and Pustay, Michael W. International Business, Six edition. Prentice Hall 2010. Chapter 4: "The Role of culture" page 89.

1. http://www.cbsnews.com/stories/2009/02/27/60minutes/main4833667.shtml
(CBS news: The Man who Figured out Madoff Scheme)

2. http://seekingalpha.com/article/212781-financial-shenanigans-shows-how-companies-try-to-hide-their-problems
(Seeking Alpha: investment website,'Financial Shenanigans' Shows How Companies Try to Hide Their Problems, Enron Scandal)

3. http://www.oxforddictionaries.com/definition/ethics?view=uk
(ethics definition)

4. http://dealbook.nytimes.com/2011/03/30/sokol-resigns-from-berkshire-hathaway/ (Abrupt Exit for a Top Deputy to Warren Buffett, New York Times)

5. http://www.pbs.org/wgbh/aia/part4/4h1549.html
(Emancipation Proclamation, Historical Document)

⇒ Akrani, Gaurav. "Planning First Primary Important Function of Management." <http://kalyan-city.blogspot.com/2010/06/planning-first-primary-important.html> Web 25 Apr. 2011.

⇒ Ansoff I. 1991. Critique of Henry Mintzberg's 'The design school: reconsidering the basic premises of strategic management.' *Strategic Management Journal.*

⇒ Armstrong J. 1982. The value of formal planning for strategic decisions: review of empirical research. *Strategic Management Joumal.*

⇒ Bracker J, Keats B, Pearson J. 1988. Planning and financial performance among small firms in a growth industry. *Strategic Management Joumal.*

⇒ Brian, Dumain. "P&G Rewrites the Marketing Rules." Fortune, November 6, 1990. p. 34.

⇒ Brews P, Hunt M. 1999. Learning to plan and planning to learn: resolving the planning school/learning school debate. *Strategic Management Joumal.*

⇒ "Get Organized: The Importance of Planning." <> Web 27 Apr. 2011.

⇒ Locke E, Latham G. 1980. *A Theory of Goal Setting and Task Performance.* Prentice-Hall: Englewood Cliffs, NJ.

⇒ McNamara, Carter. "Basic Guidelines for Successful Planning." Free Management Library. <http://managementhelp.org/plan_dec/gen_plan/gen_pl an.htm#anch or1384873> Web 25 Apr. 2011.

⇒ Robbins, Stephen P. 2002. *Management.* Prentice-Hall: Englewood Cliffs, NJ.

⇒ Robinson R. 1984. Forecasting and small business: a study of the strategic planning process. *Joumal of Small Business Management.*

⇒ Shrader C, Mulford C, Blackburn V. 1989. Strategic and operational planning, uncertainty, and performance in small firms. *Journal of Small Business Management.*

⇒ Smith K, Locke E, Barry D. 1990. Goal setting, planning, and organizational performance: an experimental simulation. *Organizational Behavior and Human Decision Processes.*

⇒ *Successful Manager's Handbook: Development Suggestions for Today's Manager.* 1989. Personnel Decisions: Minneapolis.

⇒ "Plan." Dictionary.com, n.d. Web. 28 Apr 2011. <http://dictionary. reference.com/browse/plan>.

⇒ "All About Strategic Planning." *Management Help.* Free Management Library, n.d. Web. 28 Apr 2011. <http://managementhelp.org/ plan_dec/str_plan/str_plan.htm#anchor1234>.

⇒ "Types of planning." *Center for Strategic Planning.* Plan Online, n.d. Web. 28 Apr 2011. <http://www.planonline.org/crib/types.htm>.

⇒ "Tactical Planning Vs. Strategical Planning." *Management Innovations.* Management Innovations, n.d. Web. 28 Apr 2011. <http://managementinnovations.wordpress.com/2008/12/10/ tactical-planning-vs-strategic-planning/>.

⇒ "Types of planning." *Center for Strategic Planning.* Plan Online, n.d. Web. 28 Apr 2011. <http://www.planonline.org/crib/types. htm>.

⇒ "The Strategic Planning Process." Quick MBA, n.d. Web. 29 Apr 2011. <http://www.quickmba.com/strategy/strategic-planning/>.

⇒ "Tactical Planning." Business Coaching Executive, n.d. Web. 29 Apr 2011. <http://www.businesscoachingexecutive.com/ tactical-planning>.

⇒ Schroeder, Roger. *Operations Management: Contemporary Concepts and Cases.* 4th. New York, NY: McGraw-Hill/Irwin, 2008. Print.

⇒ The Difference Between Strategic Planning and Tactical Planning http://www.morebusiness.com/strategic-planning

⇒ Strategic Planning vs. Tactical Planning by powerup. http://upwardaction.com/wordpress/2007/10/22/strategic-planning-tactical-planning/

⇒ Tips for Mentees by Linda Phillips Jones http://www.mentoringgroup.com/mentees.html

Mcnamara, Carter, and Rolfe Larson. "Business Planning (For nonprofits, for-profits and hybrid organizations)." n. pag. *Free Management Library*. Web. 25 Apr 2011. <http://managementhelp.org/plan_dec/bus_plan/bus_plan.htm>.

Mintzberg, Henry. "The Fall and Rise of Strategic Planning." 11. Web. 28 Apr 2011. <https://fhict.fontys.nl/es/MScModules/IMAN/Shared%20Documents/Fall%20and%20Rise%20of%20SP.pdf>.

(1) White, Janeth. "How to become a better planner." 5. Web. 28 Apr 2011. <http://www.docstoc.com/docs/2574006/How-to-be-a-Better-Planner>.

Whitehead, Katharine. *Component-Based Development : Principles and Planning for Business Systems*. 1. New York: Print.

⇒ "Importance of Planning." *HubPages*. Web. 29 Apr. 2011. <http://hubpages.com/hub/Importance-of-Planning>.

⇒ Judge, Timothy A. "1." *Organizational Behavior*. By Stephen P. Robbins. Fourteenth ed. 5-7. Print.

⇒ "The Planning Cycle—Project Management Tools from MindTools.com." *Mind Tools—Management Training, Leadership Training and Career Training*. Web. 29 Apr. 2011. <http://www.mindtools.com/pages/article/newPPM_05.htm>.

⇒ "Why Is Planning Important?" *Submit Articles or Find Free Articles*. Web. 29 Apr. 2011. <http://www.articlealley.com/article_32151_36.html>.

⇒ Baker, H. K., & Phillips, A. L. (1999). Career Paths of Corporate CFOs and Treasurers. *Financial Practice and Education* [the name has changed to Journal of Applied Finance], *9*(2), 38-50.

⇒ Graham, L. A., & Krueger, T. (1996). What Does a Graduate Need?: Conflict in CFO and Student Opinions. *Financial Practice and Education* [the name has changed to Journal of Applied Finance], *6*(2), 60-67.

⇒ Hayes, J. (2001). People-focused 'organizational paradigm' lets staffers shine. *Nation's Restaurant News*, *35*(4), 50.

⇒ Ricadela, A. (2000). Reich Touts The *Human Factor. Information Week*, (777), 40.

⇒ Zich, J. (1998, September). Ideas: We're All is This Together. *Stanford Business*. Retrieved August 10, 2003, from http://www.gsb.stanford.edu/community/bmag/sbsm9809/ideas.html

1- ***Seven habits of highly effective people*** by Stephen R. Covey
2- http://www.sas.calpoly.edu/asc/ssl/procrastination.html
3- http://www.time-management-improvement.com/prioritizing.html
4- **Seven habits of highly effective people** by Stephen R. Covey

	Urgent	Not Urgent
Important	**I** ACTIVITIES: Crises Pressing problems Deadline-driven projects	**II** ACTIVITIES: Prevention Relationship building Recreation New opportunities
Not Important	**III** ACTIVITIES: Interruptions Some phone calls Some mail Some meetings Popular activities	**IV** ACTIVITIES: Trivia Some mail Some phone calls Time wasters Pleasure activities

5- Lakein, Alan (1973). *How to Get Control of Your Time and Your Life*. New York: P.H. Wyden

6- http://www.dkeener.com/keenstuff/priority.html

7- http://www.mindtools.com/pages/article/newTED_02.htm

8- http://en.wikipedia.org/wiki/Time_management

9- http://michaelgreer.biz/?p=138

10- example of Prioritization Matrix chart

List of Problems	Criteria: Frequency	Criteria: Importance	Criteria: Feasibility	Total Points

11- http://www.brighthub.com/office/project-management/articles/44798.aspx

12- http://www.velaction.com/9-square-prioritization-tool/

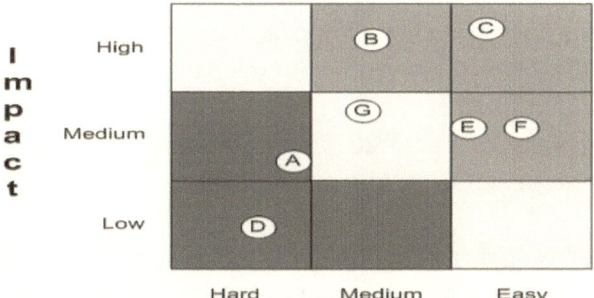

And also,
http://m2weekly.com/insight/5-simple-steps-to-becoming-a-whiz-at-prioritization/

http://wiki.answers.com/Q/What_does_priorities_means

"What does priority means?", Anonymous, Free Encyclopedia, 2011

http://ezinearticles.com/?What-Are-Priorities-And-Why-Are-They-Important?&id=582179
"What are priorities and why are they important?", Joe E. Lawrence, 2011

http://www.marin.edu/~don/Study/5time.html
"How to be successful", Donald Martin, 1991

http://www.mindtools.com/pages/article/newHTE_92.htm
"Focus on Priorities", Mind Tools

http://www.mindtools.com/pages/article/newHTE_91.htm
"Using time effectively, not just efficiently", Mind Tools

Blair, Gerard M. The Art of Delegation. n.d. 12 4 2011 <http://www.see.ed.ac.uk/~gerard/Management/art5.html>.

Businessballs. n.d. 13 4 2011 <http://www.businessballs.com/delegation.htm>.

Johnson, Lauren Keller. Working Knowledge. 6 9 2004. 11 04 2011 <http://hbswk.hbs.edu/archive/4355.html>.

MindTools. n.d. 14 04 2011 <http://www.mindtools.com/pages/article/newLDR_98.htm>.

MindTools. n.d. 16 4 2011 <http://www.mindtools.com/pages/article/newTMM_60.htm>.

Montgomery, Haley. Bright Hub. 31 10 2009. 18 04 2011 <http://www.brighthub.com/office/project-management/articles/54501.aspx>.

Mulberry. HubPages. n.d. 10 4 2011 <http://hubpages.com/hub/How-To-Delegate>.

Tyson, Bruce. <u>Bright Hub</u>. 6 9 2010. 21 4 2011 <http://www.brighthub.com/office/project-management/articles/85926.aspx>.

[1]http://www.mindtools.com/pages/article/newLDR_98.htm

[1]http://www.pmhut.com/12-rules-of-delegation

[1]http://businesspherconsulting.com/five-easy-steps-to-delegate-to-enhance-your-business—performance/

[1]http://sloanreview.mit.edu/the-magazine/1998-winter/3922/intellectual-capital-competence-x—commitment/

[1]Leadership and the One Minute Manager by Blanchard, Kenneth; Zigarmi, Patricia and Zigarmi, Drea.

[1]http://www.trainingbulletin.co.uk/resources/articles/article.php?topic_id=7

[1]http://www.g4sleader.lmmattersonline.com/courses/HMM10%20Courseware/delegating/what_not_to_delegate.html

[1]http://www.inc.com/guides/2010/04/how-to-delegate-properly.html

⇒ Author's Last Name, Author's First Name. "Book Title or Reference Title." City
⇒ Name: Publisher, Date.

(1) Wikipedia Organization. *"Recruitment Article"*. Website: http://en.wikipedia.org/wiki/Recruitment

(2) Staffing and Recruiting Specialists. *"Employee Hiring Checklist"*. Website: http://www.staffing-and-recruiting-essentials.com/Hiring-Checklist.html

(3) Wikipedia Organization. *"Training Article"*. Website: http://en.wikipedia.org/wiki/Training

(4) Knol Specialists. *"Building Effective Training in 5 Steps"*. Website: http://knol.google.com/k/building-effective-training-in-five-easy-steps#

⇒ http://www.objectivebusiness.com/index.php?module=pagemaster&PAGE_user_op=view_page&PAGE_id=8&MMN_position=12:12

⇒ http://www.more-for-small-business.com/measurebusinessperformance.html

⇒ http://www.balancedscorecard.org/BSCResources/PerformanceMeasurement/WhatShouldYouMeasure/tabid/138/Default.aspx

⇒ http://www.iusb.edu/~sbres/workshop/elements.html

⇒ Lesikar, R. V., Flatley, M. E., & Rentz, K. (2008). Business Communication: Making Connections in a Digital World. New York, NY: McGraw-Hill Irwin. http://www.blurtit.com/q680271.html

http://thinkexist.com/quotations/innovation/
http://en.wikipedia.org/wiki/Innovation

Books:
o "Developing a collection" by Elinor Renfrew & Colin Renfrew
o The teen vogue hand book: an insider's guide to careers in fashion
o www.businessdictionary.com on the word "Innovation".
o "The nature and importance of Innovation" Princeton Press. < http://press.princeton.edu/chapters/s9221.pdf>.

o   "What do Google, Apple, and Harley Davidson have in common" Innovation Zen. 2006. 29 April 2011. < http://innovationzen.com/blog/2006/10/30/what-does-google-apple-and-harley-davidson-have-in-common/>

o   Evans, Harold. "What drives America's great innovators?" Fortune Magazine 18 October 2004. 29 April 2011. <http://money.cnn.com/magazines/fortune/fortune_archive/2004/10/18/8188088/index.htm>

o   "What drives innovation?" Ideaflow. October 2004. 29 April 2011. < http://ideaflow.corante.com/archives/2004/10/14/what_drives_innovation.php>

o   "Who made America?" < http://www.pbs.org/wgbh/theymadeamerica/whomade/innovators_lo.html>

o   Jaruzelski, Barry and Mainard, Cesare R. "The World's 10 Most Innovative Companies, And How They Do It" Forbes Magazine. 4 April 2011. 29 April 2011. < http://www.forbes.com/2011/04/04/10-top-innovative-companies-apple-google-leadership-managing-how.html>

o   Gupta, Praveen. "Measures of Innovation Proposal" Innovationmetrics.gov. April 2007. 29 April 2011. <http://www.innovationmetrics.gov/comments/042707GuptaPraveen.pdf>

o   WEST'S Legal Enviroment of Business, Sixth Edition

o   Globalization and Its Impacts,www.ilo.org

o   www.wikipedia.org

o   Humphrey, B., & Stokes, J. (2000). Nine essential skills for frontline leaders. Society for Human Resource Management.

o   American heritage dictionary of the English language (4th ed.). (2003). Boston, MA: Houghton-Mifflin.

o   Cunning, S. M. (2004). Avoid common management pitfalls. Nursing Management, 35(2), 18.

o   Giuliani, R. (2002). Leadership. New York: Hyperion.

o   Freedman, D. (2000). Corps business: The 30 management principles of the U.S. Marine Corps. New York: HarperCollins Publishers.

o   Findley, H.M., & Amsler, G. (2003). Setting performance expectations: Return to the basics. Society for Human Resource Management.

o   Gish, J. (2003). Managing a professional workforce. Supervision, 64(7), 8.
o   Giuliani, R. (2002). Leadership. New York: Hyperion.
o   Humphrey, B., & Stokes, J. (2000). Nine essential skills for frontline leaders. Society for Human Resource Management.
o   Http://www.shrm.org/

Start Up Nation: the story of Israel's economic miracle, Dan Senor and Saul Singer

www.wikipedia.com
www.google.com

ABOUT THE AUTHOR

Dr. Librado E. Gonzalez, is a Global Human Resources and Operations Professional with track record of hands-on human resources operations, experienced in a multi-unit and multi-national environment. With over 20 years of experience in the field. His educational background comes from a MBA at University of Barcelona, Doctorate of Law at British American University, and a Ph.D. in Management from La Salle University, alone with Mediation Certifications from Duke University and Washington University. He is a Certified Executive Coach, a Master Six Sigma Black Belt Certified and Lean Certified Trainer. He has held executive positions within private and government organizations. He has been a Business and Law Professor for Towson University, State University of New York, Empire State College, Laurel University, Northern California University, Universidad Latina and Catawba Valley Community College. He has been a guess speaker for private and government agencies in the U.S., Latin America, Europe and Asia.

He is the author of "How to Understand Communication" 2005; "The Issues Management Book" 2008 and now "How to Become an Extraordinary Manager" 2011.

www.ingramcontent.com/pod-product-compliance
Lightning Source LLC
Chambersburg PA
CBHW032007170526

45157CB00002B/589